Roots of Open Education in America

Reminiscences and Reflections

Editors:
RUTH DROPKIN AND ARTHUR TOBIER

THE CITY COLLEGE WORKSHOP CENTER FOR
OPEN EDUCATION
New York, New York 10031   December 1976

THE CITY COLLEGE WORKSHOP CENTER FOR OPEN EDUCATION, founded in 1972, is a free facility for all teachers, administrators, paraprofessionals, and parents who are interested and involved in open education in the New York City area. Its work is supported by funds from the Far West Laboratory for Educational Research and Development, National Institute of Education, Rockefeller Brothers Fund, and City College. Its director is Lillian Weber.

Room 6, Shepard Hall, City College
Convent Avenue and 140th Street
New York, New York 10031

© 1976 by the Workshop Center for Open Education

Library of Congress Number: 76-531-46

ISBN: 0-918374-01-4

ACKNOWLEDGMENTS

To *Lillian Weber*, who pioneered in open education for the public schools of America, and who had the idea for the conference from whose proceedings this book is drawn;

To *Marian Brooks*, who, as head of the elementary education department at City College, supported the first Open Corridor developments, and whose 50th anniversary as a teacher and trainer of teachers was saluted at the occasion on April 12, 1975;

To the *participants* at the City College all-day meeting, whose wholehearted endorsement encouraged us to undertake this publication;

To *Vicki Reed*, who searched out, annotated, and arranged the conference photo exhibit from which this book's illustrations were selected, and to *Yvette LeRoy* of the Schomburg Library, *Leroy Bellamy* and *Jerry Kearns* of the Library of Congress, and *Charlotte LaRue* of the Museum of the City of New York, who assisted;

To *Gertrude Herman*, Librarian at the University of Wisconsin in Madison, and to those conference speakers who contributed to the Bibliography for this volume;

To *Rachel Aaron, Nora Moran*, and *Barbara Owens*, who transcribed tapes and typed final copy;

To the *National Endowment for the Humanities,* the *North Dakota Study Group on Evaluation,* and the *Rockefeller Brothers Fund,* whose financial assistance made this publication possible.

LIST OF ILLUSTRATIONS

Cover: Children playing in front of a settlement house in New York City. Late 1800s. Jacob Riis Collection, Museum of the City of New York

Following page 12: Contraband School
Harriet Murray

Following page 32: Settlement House Playground
Immigrant Class

Following page 58: Sod Schoolhouse
Salter School
Blanche Lamont School

Following page 72: Moonlight School
Corn Offering

Following page 90: Jim Walker
Star Pupil

Following page 130: Friedrich Froebel
Boston Kindergarten

Following page 147: F.E.R.A.
War Nursery

Following page 190: Bringing in the Apple Crop
Building with Blocks

CONTENTS

Introduction • *Lillian Weber* 1
Akwesasne Education • *Sakakohe Cook* 7
Pre- and Post-Emancipation Schools • *Osborne E. Scott* 13
Workers Education • *Mark Starr; Julius Manson* 21
Settlement Houses • *Helen Hall; H. Daniel Carpenter* 33
The *Shule* • *Louis Cohen* 42
Developing a New Educational Agenda • *David Hawkins* 49
The One-Room Schoolhouse — South • *Mary Burks* 59
The One-Room Schoolhouse — North • *Neva Larocque Howrigan* 67
Highlander • *Myles Horton; Claudia Lewis* 73
The WPA Experience • *Edward Glannon* 91
Citizenship Schools • *Dorothy Cotton; Myles Horton* 101
Dewey's Synthesis: Science and Feeling • *Joseph Featherstone* 118
Some Economic Questions • *Paul Nash* 126
Early Progressive Schools — I • *Neith Headley* 131
Early Progressive Schools — II • *Charlotte B. Winsor* 135
The First Day Care Program • *Cornelia Goldsmith* 148
Residential Programs • *Walter E. Clark; Vincent Wright* 161
A View of School Reform • *Vito Perrone* 173
Bibliography • *Marian Brooks* 191
Contributors 198

The April 12, 1975 Conference on the Roots of Open Education in America was an event of high drama, both in its creation and in its effect. In the preparation, as one name led to another, as telephone calls and letters crossed the country, old connections between people and programs were revived, and new connections established. At the conference itself, unforeseen reunions—in the audience and at the podium—were often moving and memorable. In these pages, we present the day's highlights, fully aware that the conference was but a beginning, and its proceedings a small sample. Had we had the resources in money and staff, we could have tapped more sources and pursued more leads. As it is, we hardly touched the western experience and not at all, to our regret, the Hispanic. The task of exploring and reviving and reinforcing all our roots remains to be done.

Introduction

LILLIAN WEBER

Why a conference on the Roots of Open Education in the spring of 1975 and why one that had the particular shape of this one? What did we, working in a framework collectively identified, for better or worse, as open education, hope to clarify beyond what was already obvious to many of us—namely, that so much of the discussion about open education to that point seemed to fall within the absurd context of "new developments," without a history or a past. What beyond the fact that many of us saw a clear need for a revival of the past as a living force to be interpreted and reinterpreted? We knew that we needed to reconnect to our past, but which past? And for what meanings of open education?

From what past had I drawn my own commitments? Were they indeed derived, as I had reported, from my study of institutional examples and theoretical formulations of progressive education, my study at the Bank Street College of Education, my work as a nursery school teacher? Certainly these were resources on which I drew. In fact, with so little in contemporary psychological research showing any awareness of the continuities in children's development, as well as of the function of time, I had found it necessary to reexamine the serious longitudinal child development studies from Iowa, Merrill-Palmer, Bank Street, the Dewey School experience.

What I recognized in these studies of informal education and in ideas generally embodied by informal education, was the context of life as it existed for me in my childhood. It existed for me in my memories of kitchen smells—of baked apples and rice pudding, of all of us working at our different things at the round oak table, under the hanging lamp. Where and when did I begin to feel for the natural world? My memories—always with my father or an older brother or sister—are of dew, of early morning mists, of first swimming, of the harvest moon blood-red and hanging low. It was with all these memories that I resonated to the truth of the description of prior-to-school learning. If I had not recognized the roots in life itself, my Bank Street studies would have remained disembodied theory.

As I talked with parents about open education, they all, in greater or lesser degree, expressed these recognitions too: the bypassing incidental focus, the intimacies, the awareness—in all families of more than one child—of difference, of sense of place and acceptance, of being included, of continuity in relatedness. All of this they saw as the stuff of the prior-to-school context.

For myself as middle child in a big family, perhaps more had existed than such generalized and universal aspects of prior-to-school learning. I remember that there was *room* for me to be reflective about my place in the family. I was allowed to present a "stone-face" to the enormously rich life around me, *while* I made an effort to understand it. Our household was based on respect for the person; the constant self-assessment and examination of ideas and of personality and character differences in the household was a conscious teaching environment.

There was a very strong assumption in my family, perhaps because of its size, of diversity and difference among all of us. Certainly, one had to get along in this family, but the idea of adjusting to some standard did not exist in quite the way it is discussed today. In my family, strong support for and loyalty to each other and to the family were taken for granted, but apparently differences could exist within this extremely strong social framework.

I remembered other experiences, all voluntary, all external to school structures—each of us choosing from the array of offerings during the two weeks of Chautauqua, when I lived in West Virginia, and then the discussions that followed for many more weeks. I remember my father's comments on labor schools, his own education through union work, the experiences I heard described, when I lived in Virginia, of those who worked with the Highlander Folk School, discussions about how to fight the poll tax and about rural electrification. There was even more in the surroundings of my growing-up years than the intimacies I later recognized when reading the descriptions that bolstered discussions of developmental theory. There were the recognitions of my immigrant family culture in the books I read. The literary societies described in *The Little House on the Prairie* had their parallel in the Jewish P.E.N. clubs that welcomed recitals of my mother's poetry. My mother, who was a child of her culture, spoke to us about the dancer Isadora Duncan and the cause of freedom and expression for the human body. She would illustrate a point with the work of those writers who were important to her—Tolstoy, Heine, Hugo. Though she was not at all interested in politics, she knew what was going on; the struggles and strivings of this or that group were alive in my household.

Understanding was a big word in my family. I was strongly conscious at all times of *trying* to understand, of striving to make sense. Education equated with understanding went on at all times—at the table, in walks, in all aspects of life. But I'm sure this consciousness about education was not a characteristic of my family alone. It was probably strong in all my parents' generation who were seeking to better things, who had to set up their own newspapers, their own voluntary societies, their own institutions to accomplish this. My father and his generation in the late 19th century were steeped in a rationalism and in a belief in progress and democracy that was based on the assertion of human potential, of human understanding. In my home it was assumed that people were intelligent, that they were strong and capable, and that all were entitled to the dignity of man.

Thus the continuities within the ideas of progressive education and the cultural context of my growing up are obvious. How could I not, drawing on such recollections, find obvious resonances in the later discussions on language acquisition, comprehension, I.Q.; the assumption of intelligence is central to my own system of values. In the years I studied informal education in England, I was not surprised to discover that Robert Owen, a socialist, reacted to the horrors of the Industrial Revolution with a search for ways that would support the development of the potential in all children, for ways that could include *all* children in the enjoyment of their own childhood. I was not surprised that Susan Isaacs and the McMillan sisters, who picketed Parliament in 1917 for free nursery schools, also sought ways of making the world better: a standard of inclusiveness that embraced the right of all children to express their potentiality. That the kindergartens of Caroline Pratt and of the Ethical Culture Societies served the children of working class families, and that they were organized for the purpose of being inclusive rather than exclusive, struck me as entirely natural.

What was it about these earlier experiences that related them to my later study? What indeed was central to these experiences and the development of open education? The community? The preservation of the cultural inheritance? The intergenerational character of the experiences? All these, and more, for inherent in all was an offering of educative experience to the learner without sorting mechanisms or certification systems or prior qualifications. Indeed, as I mulled over the experiences I had culled from my memories, it struck me how such offerings and such a welcome to the willing learner seemed to be the expectation of many groups in their vision of America, particularly the immigrants who, in their coming, challenged the deference to class and educational status and asserted themselves as people with potential. They organized cultural experiences to sustain themselves in this strange land; they joined educational enterprises—literary societies, singing clubs, and so on—to help map their own path to self-fulfillment, without old-world constraints. They, of course, used the public schools, as well as these extra-school experiences, but it is clear from the number of communal educational groups that the schools provided insufficient nutrients for the ordinary person's drive for further development and cultural continuity.

It was confidence in the human as learner that inspired progressive educators; it was the natural ways in which human learning developed which they studied in their effort to revitalize the schools. Whatever their nationality—Froebel, Pestalozzi, Montessori—they drew on what they knew of the learner, as observed in informal settings—family experiences and the communal cultural experiences—and they tried to figure out how to plan for, maintain, and keep continuous the vigor of this informal learning, within the schools. The sensitive educators who planned the Dewey School, for instance, observing that for the American child of the late 19th and early 20th centuries the informal educative experiences in the pre-industrial frontier household were less available, attempted to revive their nutritive force in the learning process by including them in schools.

The ideas of open education, after all, are about person, about difference, about continuity, about human striving to make both sense of the world and an impact on it, about potentiality and the conditions of life that nurture or suppress the flowering of potentiality, about the conditions that allow the recognition and emergence of ideas, and about the professional, theoretical, and institutional context of schooling. What is inherent to open education understood in this way is a broad acceptance of all humans as part of the group and value and respect for all persons as active learners, capable of intelligent, active efforts to survive. It followed naturally for us to value stories of human experience—even more, stories of immigrant survival and the self-assertion of the oppressed. In these informal, historical accounts, whether novelistic or autobiographical—accounts of how each group, or each family unit, struggling to survive, organized cultural and personal experiences to sustain and fulfill a way of life—we found the roots of open education. And out of this understanding, which has blown life into our work at the Workshop Center for Open Education, we organized our conference. The all-day meeting, which drew an audience of more than 500 people, was a dramatic and often stirring convergence of old and young—those in the vanguard of today's efforts to restore humanistic values to schools as well as spokespersons for similar but older, even vanished, currents in American life.

Nor was this conference simply a nostalgia trip. Its evocation of the past was organized with the idea of confirming the continuity of those strands in our national life that encouraged self-development. By bringing together people whose experiences in informal organizations appeared to reinforce the truth about our contemporary belief in human educability, the conference hoped to reaffirm the humanist wellspring of America. It created the opportunity for firsthand encounters with men and women who had played a vital part in programs predicated on faith in the educability of *all* people. Through informal, small-group interchanges, conference participants experienced the excitement of sharing in living history. Their sense of renewal flowed from the spirit and substance of the presentations they heard. What they were treated to was genuine oral history about persons, times, and ideas whose meaning, often overlooked, obscured or bypassed, was this day given new life. Their appreciation was succinctly expressed by one participant:

> When I thought back over the day it struck me very forcibly: There is no culture without history. History gives feelings of connectedness, it refreshes you and lifts you.

Akwesasne Education

The symbol of the Iroquois Confederacy is a pine tree. That pine tree has an eagle on the top, since the eagle can fly higher and see further than any other bird.... That pine tree has four white roots. Those roots go to the four directions and they grow ... if the people want to follow those roots and to trace the roots back to the tree, under which they can sit and be sheltered from the hot sun and from the cold winds, they can sit there in peace with our Confederacy.

SAKAKOHE COOK • I am from the Wolf Clan of the Mohawk Nation of the Iroquois Confederacy. I have found, in speaking with people such as yourselves, that there are few who actually know anything about us. Having gone through the American school system, primarily the Catholic school system, I found that to be so. My knowledge comes from living with my parents, with my grandparents, with my people. I apologize to you that the other representatives from home are not here. I'll try to speak, as they've asked me to, saying, "Saka, you go and you tell them what they need to know and what they want to know. And remember that you're speaking from home."

When I got here, I walked around and saw the beautiful exhibit of pictures. One picture also had some words, and part of those words says, "The four main objectives of elementary education in America are (1) to help children learn how to get along with other people, (2) to protect and maintain their health, (3) to learn the wise use of their leisure time, and (4) to develop the skills and understanding needed to solve the problems of their homes, their community, and their own individual lives." As I read this, I began thinking how very curious it was that these were the main objectives of elementary education, because to me, the way I was brought up, those are the main objectives of the family.

I hold a very different place in my home than is traditional. I am one of the few Mohawk women who, only a few years ago, left the reserve to become educated. It's not quite as strange now. But at the time, I was one of those very, very few people who were female and who went out and got this thing called a B.A. I call it strange because when I go home they say to me, "Saka, we're going to have to watch you very carefully because you've been out there and you've been educated by those white people." Now, I know that a person grows up learning and being what the influences are. I learned from watching your faces and, later, from hearing your voices today; part of you becomes me. In the same way, your children are what you taught them. So I look at this, and I hear them at home, and they say to me, "Because of that experience on the outside, you have got somewhere in your head the influence of those white people. And we want to make sure that you haven't forgotten who Saka Cook is." Now they know that they don't have to be quite as careful because they've watched me and they've seen how I've grown.

This place—this conference—is called "The Roots of Open Education." The word "roots" in there really attracted me. The symbol of the Iroquois Confederacy is a pine tree. That pine tree has an eagle at the top, since the eagle can fly higher and see farther than any other bird. If there are any problems coming, that eagle will tell us. That pine tree has four white roots. At the time of the founding of the Confederacy, it was said, as it is said now, that those white roots will go to the four corners of the world to teach people about the Confederacy. And if the people want to follow those roots and to trace the roots back to the tree, under which they can sit and be sheltered from the hot sun by its limbs, be sheltered from the winds that can be cold, they can sit there in peace with our Confederacy.

For those of you who don't know—and to remind those of you who do—we're still very much alive. We number probably more than we did at the time that this man, Christopher Columbus, accidentally came over here and decided he was in

India. We are the fastest growing minority in the United States and we intend keeping that race record because we know that it is important for us to be here.

David Hawkins referred to the "custodians of the planet." At first, in the context of all the names he mentioned and the words he used, I was left unclear about his meaning. But then I thought: I hear the same thing at home. What they mean at home when they say "custodians of the earth" is not the same as, say, my being custodian of a cup, because it's not my cup, it is its own cup. So I have no right to the custodial ownership of it. But I do have the obligation to make sure that this cup is not mistreated. I also have, as a woman, and some day I hope as a mother, the same obligation to my children and to my grandchildren. I owe them the obligation of these four things that I read to you earlier, as well as all of the other things that enter into this thing called "education."

I wasn't around when the Confederacy was formed, and I'm not exactly positive how it was that they taught their children, who are my grandfathers. My heart tells me that they were taught in much the same way that my grandmother taught me. That way was simply by watching and doing, watching for the first few minutes and after that doing. She made donuts not by sitting and looking at a recipe of how to make donuts, but by waking up at 5 o'clock on a Tuesday morning and making them; by waking up and going down there and frying eight dozen donuts in one hour, by making sure that you got the next 20 dozen in the next three hours. I learned by sitting combing her hair and listening to the stories of her childhood—in the same way that many of you at some point have experienced the learning of your grandparents and, I hope, of your parents. To me that's where education belongs—in the home.

Somewhere in my education, one of my professors said that the reason public education was started in the United States was to make sure that the values of the larger society were known to the children, so that there would be a natural process of pulling it together and so that they would be loyal to this country. The larger society could bring them all up and they'd be the same: there'd be equal and free opportunity in education regardless of race, color, and creed.

Words. It doesn't work, I don't think. At least, I haven't seen it work for me and for my people.

For us, education from Europe came when we first made contact with Europeans in the form of missionaries. In our case, they were the Jesuits. Lots of books have been written about the Mohawk nation; I remember, in reading those books, always seeing us referred to as "those savages." The same was true of my history books and is true of the books your children are reading. One of the earliest thoughts was that we were not educable, because, after all, we were animals, without souls. Of course, I realize now that we had to be animals without souls because you can't do those things to a people who are your equal. That creates guilt and guilt is something to be avoided. One has to provide for one's own needs, say the Europeans. And then one says, "Okay, there is not much land here in Europe; we can't make a living here. On the other hand, there's nobody using the whole northern continent of this New World. The people there, my goodness, they're not people. They don't wear clothes; they're bloodthirsty savages. We're going to go over and tame them."

Now, if anyone said to me, "Saka, give me one word that best describes Mohawk," I would have to say *respect*. It is our way to listen to people—it is ingrained in us. If it's the missionary coming in to talk about a God, well and good. We knew about God; maybe theirs and ours were the same. Well, the missionaries took it a step further. They knew that, as one writer put it, "You can't teach Indians all about Europe if they're among their own kind because they remain the dirty savages that they are." So they decided to take a few boys and girls and start a school with them in Connecticut, a charity school, Wheeler by name, I think, just prior to the founding of Dartmouth College. The missionaries decided—and I would imagine that if this was done once it was done many times—that if they could take a youth and expose him during that impressionable age to all of the wonders and the beauty and the superiority of European culture, that child might somehow get over being the savage that he was born to be.

One of the things mandated by the scholarship that was established was that the children live with a white family for three years afterwards. They figured if we can make those children turn into men who know the white world, when we send them home they'll live longer because they'll know how to live in that atmosphere. They'll speak English and they'll also speak their native language, so they won't have that problem. And because they are Mohawk or Seneca or Cayuga, the people will listen to them. But that didn't work. When that child returned home, the people watched that child the same way my people watched me when I got out of college, except it wasn't the same. The child had become used to living in a house and wearing shoes, used to hearing the English language. All of those things and all of the subtleties that occur when you're exposed to another world. In his head, the person was no longer "Mohawk." Perhaps he was in his heart, but it has to be the two. That was the transitional period.

Now the cycle is going back. Now we are hoping in the next few years to establish the second Mohawk Way school. We've tried one and we've learned from that that we have to make some refinements, to find yet another way. Akwesasne today has about 6,000 people on it. It averages out to about 10 acres to a person. Very swampy, so that my 10 acres may be something that I can't even walk on or at least live on. But we know who we are. The Mohawk language is the functional language. Even the Mass is said in Mohawk. The longhouse is still there. Our ceremonies are still there. And, most important, our grandparents are still there, for it is the grandparents who have the time to teach the children. It is the grandparents who have just enough of that removal and all of that love and all of that wisdom to teach the children. That can happen sometimes with the parents, but it's not the same thing. The parents have to be too concerned with all of the other facets of all of the children. But it's the grandparents who give us our strength. It's they who watch and say, "Saka Cook, we want you to finish school because we think that you'll come out okay. We're watching you."

The important thing with us, the way we have always learned, is through the voice—the voice that comes from the mind and the heart. We have an oral tradition, which is why grandparents are so important. In the stories, in the legends, in the wampum belts are contained all of our history, all of our knowledge. The Mohawk Way school decided that it was important for the children to know these things just as it is now important for them to know how to read, write, and do math. So a couple of the traditional parents got together and arranged to have a certified teacher—since New York State demands a certified teacher—come to teach the children all of the things inherent in those belts, in those songs, in those legends.

The first Mohawk Way school didn't represent a lot of children, maybe 20, and from all ages, and sometimes they would come from the other school after 3 p.m. They came according to whatever arrangement was easiest for them. But one of the proudest days I've ever had came from going over to that school one night. A little child, about six, and with those beautiful eyes of his, came up to me and said, "Saka Cook, can you read this belt to me?" I looked at him and said, "All I can read is the first half of it. Will you tell me the rest?" And that six-year-old read the rest of that belt to me. It was astounding.

A contraband school during the Civil War. "Contraband" was the term used to describe slaves who escaped to, or were brought within, Union lines. Schomburg Library.

Harriet W. Murray instructing Elsie and Puss in the Sea Islands, South Carolina, where teachers flocked during the Civil War to set up schools for blacks within Union-occupied territory. The schools were later included in the program of the Freedmen's Bureau. Schomburg Library.

Pre- and Post-Emancipation Schools

In the post-Emancipation schools, black history was taught very early.... In fact, one of the major differences between black southern education and black northern education is that the northern black has not had that background in his own history. In many southern schools, this history was a required subject. Learning one's history was part of the process of helping people overcome the experience of being demeaned.

OSBORNE SCOTT • There has been an explosion in materials published recently dealing with black history and slavery, and the explosion in many cases has been produced by instant scholars who are designing their material to meet the public's demand for information. Many scholars in black history are extremely disturbed not only by this sudden interest of publishing companies, which is based on profit-making and aims at the commercial market, but also by the resulting distortions. An example of what I have in mind is a book that has come up with the conclusion that the slave was not subjected to as difficult an adjustment procedure as we have thought. The book claims that his life was relatively easy, that he ate the best of food and slept in dormitories, that his family life was rather fixed, and so on. To my mind, these are pure distortions, disturbing at best. There is an attempt now, among scholars, to get back to what was the essence of life under slavery, and to try to understand what the environment was, what the problems of living in the environment were. By considering how difficult it was to establish some process of education, some way for supporting people who were taken from their environment, taken forcibly, and thrust into a new culture, I think there's an opportunity to understand some of the issues underlying the whole institution of slavery, what it imposed upon the people.

Education, of course, is a process of learning. That doesn't necessarily mean a formal structure, a formal situation. Under slavery, it meant a process of accommodating oneself to an agenda that hadn't been formalized, nor necessarily organized by specialists trying to set up a curriculum. The agenda was based on a need to prepare people to survive. Dr. John Henrik Clarke, the eminent black historian, recently provided what I think is an important insight into this process of accommodation, and the strength that it took to make.

> Try to put yourself in the place of the African, taken out of his environment and brought here to circumstances beyond the imagination. If you look at the ship records and see the numbers of people crammed into those ships, and the numbers who were finally discharged, or who were finally taken off the ship when it reached here, you get some idea of the tremendous hardship under which these people came.

People were lost many times, they died of illness or committed suicide, they suffered from exposure. Up to 60 percent were not able to be put into production as slaves. The ship records that were kept indicate the trial, the strain that these people had to undergo in making this transition. We'd have an even clearer picture of this agony if we knew the numbers of people who died in the process of being taken from the interior to the slave ships on the coast. There are no such records, of course, but try to imagine it. As Clarke said in conclusion, to paraphrase him: The very fact of survival is an indication of tremendous strength. The very fact of survival.

Well, one of the processes of survival was, and has been, education and learning. The slave coming into this environment had to learn the best he could. First of all, he had to learn how to be a slave. He wasn't trained for this. He came from a background that was as varied as many aspects of our culture. He was a businessman, he was a farmer, he was a fisherman, he was a teacher, he was an artisan, he was a soldier, he was a priest, he was a government official, he was a philosopher, he was an artist, and then he had been made a slave. That involved a process of transition, which he had to learn. The education here is a little different from the education that we are talking about generally, at this conference, but it was, nevertheless, education. That process of education, moreover, was tied to the process of demeaning you. The African had to lose his sense of freedom, his sense of worth, a sense of dignity, a sense of importance. Now he had to learn that he existed only as an instrument in this *profit-making* institution, an instrument of production, a thing, property whose will was not his own. What he would learn and what he needed to learn was based definitely on his role in this environment.

Now, to jump back in time briefly in order to fill in our context, it needs to be said that freedom wasn't something that came out of the issuance of a document. It came as a result of generations of development, of a concept growing, a process of education. The people who, for many reasons, came to this country from Europe brought with them much of this tradition and heritage. But the need to develop the land, to make it productive, posed for them a great dilemma. They had to have workers. The Africans weren't the first to be used. The colonists tried first to enlist the Indian, who, as you know, resisted for many reasons. Then the European peasant was brought over under bondage, which meant that he worked for so many years, at the end of which he was free to acquire land, and so forth. But to get these people, these peasants, in the first place, as we know from history, prisons were raided and people were kidnapped off the streets. In other words, people had to be brought over forcibly, one way or another. For many reasons, this system did not work; it wasn't adequate. People couldn't be made to and wouldn't stay on the land. So the colonists turned to the African, the third man. He was used as a last resort. The introduction of guns into the world, to which the slave traders had ample access, unbalanced the equation. Nations which in the past could have defended their people were now left helpless to defend them, and their people were taken. An estimated 50 million people were lost to Africa in the slave trade, one-third of whom died between the point of their capture and the journey to the coast, one-third who, according to scholarly sources, died between the coast and the time they were entered into the slave force, and one-third who finally entered slavery. Who were these people and what were their problems?

The advent of the African slave in America created a dilemma. First of all, it challenged the history of the struggle for freedom and the whole process of acquiring a sense of worth, which was based on Judeo-Christian ethics. Secondly, it challenged a fundamental view of education, or more specifically, our attitude toward the person to be educated, which depended on our whole concept of what we think the person is, and his capacity to be educated. In order to resolve this dilemma, and the guilt that grew from it, the African had to be considered different from the ordinary person. After all, if you were led to believe that the rights of man were inalienable, yours because you were alive, then what were you going to do with this person who came into your society to be used as property, and who was not going to be accorded the status of a person? So the African came to be considered by a measure to be uneducable, or, at the least, not quite capable of being educated as everyone else with the same type of training. Even Thomas Jefferson felt that while the African could be taught to do manual things, he was not quite ready for dealing with philosophical subjects. Those who could, like Benjamin Banneker, who was a. mathematician and a publisher, were explained away as exceptions. If a slave was capable of more than manual labor, the slaveholder reasoned, it was because somewhere his blood had mixed with the European's.

It was, to say it again, what you saw of this man that determined how you were going to educate him. The Puritans had a very liberal attitude towards education and the education of the slaves. Nothing existed preventing such education for the slave or prohibiting it. However, not surprisingly, education for them meant primarily religious education, instruction in the Bible. Since the slaves were potential church members, much of the early educational efforts were given over to preaching and teaching the catechism, and so forth. The African was able to achieve some rudimentary education as a result of this. In some instances, he was able to learn to read and write. Some of the colonists who had begun as early as 1674 to set up schools for Indians began to turn their attention to the African. The feeling was that the African had to be prepared for the religious life; *that* had to be made available to him.

John Elliot was one of the first to plan a school for slaves. He had asked that masters within a radius of two or three miles send their slaves to him once a week for instruction. But Elliot died before he had the chance to put his plan fully into being. His plan had to be carried out by Cotton Mather. In Virginia, around that same time, the Anglican Church had insisted that taxes be levied against the master of every household for educating all members of his household, including his slaves. Again, that meant the education provided was to make that person effective in whatever role he had. The slave, thus, was exposed to a great deal of apprenticeship training; he was given periods of time under the tutelage of the people who had the skills he needed to learn. In addition, the Virginia colony had a population of free blacks who also had to be educated to function in the society. The free black, who came to America as an indentured servant, serving seven years usually before being freed from service and permitted to own his own land, predated the system of perpetual indenture by some 40 years. There was quite a large population of free blacks around Virginia, many of whom were the descendants of those who had been given their freedom after a period of indenture. These people, too, had to be educated. Out of this need, part and parcel of the Abolitionist movement, came the establishment of the Africa Free School, which in fact was the forerunner of free public school education.

These Africa Free Schools began in several areas, the first in New York, organized by the Mission Society in 1786. It was called Africa Free School #1 and located at 245 William Street in what is now the Wall Street area. The Mission Society had then recently organized for the purpose of doing several things: first, to lobby for laws for the emancipation of the slaves; second, to help protect runaway slaves and free blacks from being recaptured or kidnapped and resold into slavery; and, third, for the education of such slaves. These Africa Free Schools were started by people who, first of all, were convinced that the African could be educated, and who were willing to contribute money to organize such a school. Two of the prominent Americans on the board of trustees of that first Africa School were Alexander Hamilton and John Jay.

The school, of course, taught manual skills, but it also taught English grammar, mathematics, astronomy, geography, the use of maps, linear drawing for the boys. The girls were exposed to basically the same instruction, but in addition were given sewing instruction.

These were free schools for the blacks long before there was any such thing as free schools for the whites. Part of the procedure was to have periodic examinations in which the students of these schools were exposed to questions, and so forth, from the public, as a means of evaluating the effectiveness of the program. And the reports from those who took part in such evaluating sessions were simply glorious: about how intelligent the students were, and how much information they had grasped.

By 1834, seven of these schools existed. The State Legislature had granted them a budget of about a thousand dollars a year, which, at that time, was a considerable sum. They were clearly here to stay. The amount of education provided there was simply phenomenal for the time. Many of those who went through the schools went on to universities and then themselves became leaders in the Abolitionist movement.

The next phase of education for the blacks was the day schools established during the Civil War, a good example of which was the one established on St. Helena, one of the islands off the coast of South Carolina. Public education on St. Helena began one hot June morning in 1862, when a dear old lady sat with nine women in the back room of the Oakes plantation house and shared their first experience in a classroom. These pupils were ex-slaves. There were 47 eventually, all adults. And then they also began to send their children to school. Something was said this morning, at the conference, which has given some the impression that open education is a recent development; it's not. The ex-slaves had open classroom education at St. Helena, dealing with those areas that were essential for their own survival. By doing woodwork, they learned math: counting wooden logs, working at a problem in upholstery. We call it environmental math. Grandfathers taught their grandsons how to weave, a skill for which they drew on their background; they were dedicated teachers.

Following the Civil War and following these new day schools came the black colleges—Hampton, Tuskegee, Fiske, Howard, and others, set up to provide again the type of education required to help people, now free, accommodate themselves to their new environment. Education became very early a priority for the black citizen. The number of people who were educated in that brief span of time of the Reconstruction period following the Civil War was simply amazing. These schools, by the way, were the first to emphasize a vocational educational program. Many of the Polytechnic Institutes that were founded later took these earlier schools as models. Booker T. Washington, Stuart Hampton, and Frederick Hampton established Tuskegee as a model training ground in agricultural sciences. At the same time, Howard University was established to train people not only to do manual labor but also to become doctors and lawyers.

These post-Emancipation schools needed to undo the effects of the previous 100 years of education which was so demeaning. And that was done, I think, in a very interesting way. You educated the hand, the head, and the heart, as Booker T. Washington put it. Washington was severely criticized by some for this. But what he said really is that when you are able to master certain skills, and to be productive, then that in itself gives you a sense of dignity and worth. That added to self. That was basic to achieving the change in status or self-concept from one demeaned by slavery to being master of one's own mind and pocket. The process of being made a free man was composed not only of the acquiring of education but the acquiring of land. "Get a place of your own," Washington urged. "This is yours." It is amazing to consider, but, as a people, blacks own less land today, almost 50 percent less, than we did in 1900. And that's a tragedy.

In the post-Emancipation schools, black history was taught very early. I went to Hampton and came through the elementary school, so I knew black history. It was taught in the second grade and on up, as I remember. I learned about Toussaint L'Ouverture and others. In fact, one of the major differences between black southern education and black northern education is that the northern black has not had that background in his own history. In many of the southern schools, this history was a required subject. Learning one's history was part of the process of helping people overcome the experience of being demeaned.

This awareness of history as central to the education process had its roots in African tradition. In this tradition, each tribe has its historian, who is responsible for knowing the tribe's history and passing it down from family to family. It was an oral tradition that slavery failed to interrupt, the slave's rich legacy continuing with the grandparents *telling* their children. In the pre-Civil War period, it was the grandmother, or the older woman in the family, who took care of the children, who very early imparted much of this information. So you had that. That plus the fact that you had black teachers and a segregated school: you could put this awareness into being.

To repeat what I touched on earlier, in summation, the conscience that the colonialists brought into the period of slavery required the assumption that the slave learner was somehow different from other learners. This is a concept that still has great currency in presentday education. And the real dilemma is that it is entrenched in the culture. To me, it is just as much of a crack in the structure of the society as the crack in the Liberty Bell. Much of the struggle for freedom now is a struggle to overcome this basic concept which has prevailed. If you go through your country schools, you can see it. Attitudes towards children are based on our collective concept of what a child is. This has been inherited, it's part of our conditioning. But when you are also conditioned to deal with such concepts as the freedom of man and the rights of man, you've got to make some modifications in your beliefs. That sets up a dilemma that has psychological, as well as political and social, implications.

Workers Education

It is chiefly at their own union classes that the garment workers learn about the courage and daring of Clara Lemlich and her fellow waistmakers in 1909, and the awful tragedy of the Triangle fire in New York City in 1911.

MARK STARR ● What is workers education? I use the old well-worn story to define what workers education is, a story which you've probably heard. The home economics class teacher is busily showing how a few bones bought at the butcher for a few cents make the most nutritious soup. She boils the bones this-a-way and that-a-way and at the end, like all good teachers, she stops to say "any questions?" And so, of course, a Scottish lady rises up in the back and says, "But who has the meat off those bones in the first place?" I think that's as good a definition of workers education as you can get. Worker education should ask probing questions. It should be a challenge to the establishment. It should prepare the workers to be more effective in their present organization. It should build the future within the skeleton of the old establishment, preparing the worker for emancipation. Education for emancipation—that is your true beginning to workers education, as I define it.

I left school in 1907 and never even made high school. Education never interfered with my learning. But I've written books and, of course, I've had the pleasure of my associations with Dewey and the Brookwood College of Labor, a two-year college for workers that A. J. Muste started in 1921 out in Katonah, New York. It lasted until 1937, and people like the Reuther brothers and Clinton Golden came out of it. Well, in 1907, I started work and I've been doing it ever since.

I think I would describe myself as a scientific socialist

rather than a libertine liberal. There is no way out other than some basic change. I'm only hoping that a by-product of the present depression might be what it was back in the early 1930s—workers education, under the WPA, extended in a way it has never, never been extended since. Workers education is being taught now in the industrial relations department, the human relations department. What does "human relations" mean? Is there anything that exists that isn't human relations? It's a nice, amorphous title if you want to talk about what you're interested in.

At any rate, there are some unions that are doing very definite work. If you want to study what workers education did preliminary to the CIO, read a book called, *Conflict Within the AFL*. It has a whole chapter on Brookwood and workers education—why it affected the big locals of the AFL in those days, and what the struggle was about. This book is not as well known as it should be. You can get it through Cornell University Press or in libraries. Read that and also read *Essays on A. J. Muste* by Nat Hentoff.

The first time I got to know about workers education was at Ruskin College at Oxford, England. The idea at Ruskin was not to raise yourself as an individual, but to raise the class to which you belonged. Ruskin was going to educate the workers' representatives, the activists from the trades unions. But things happened there. It had a principal named Dennis Herr, who wrote one of the most attractive picture books on evolution that I've ever seen. He also committed a crime by writing a book called *A Christian With Two Wives*. If he'd written *A Christian With Two Breweries,* or *A Christian With Two Sweatshop Factories,* it would have been quite in order. But a Christian with two wives was unorthodox back in 1908 and 1909. So he got fired and the students empathized with him and went on strike. This was the first student strike on record. Workers education was more or less imported from Great Britain from that point on.

I came to the United States in 1928. I had been to Soviet Russia and I'd seen them building a new society by force and I saw the penalties that they paid. In the 1920s, the United States was supposed to be a paradise; even the intellectuals were fooled. They talked about the permanent plateau of prosperity that was being achieved here. I was curious to know about it. Henry Ford was paying $5 a day and when you translated that into pounds, shillings, and pence, it sounded like a lot of money. And, oh, all of the employers in the United States were so educated that they knew if they wanted a good labor force they had to pay a good price for it. You didn't have to go out on strike. You were sitting on an escalator and automatically wages went up. I don't need to tell you that the reality was very, very different. I went down and saw the sharecroppers. I went into the meat factory where they used everything, including the pig's squeal. I went through the automobile factories and saw the ingenuity of the assembly line and things of that sort. And before I really caught my breath, the Depression came in 1929.

I found it harder to be poor in the United States than in any other country in the world. In France, or Germany, or Britain, you had schemes for social security, and the underwriting of unemployment costs and so forth, for many, many years. But here, we just passed it on until the New Deal came along. During that time I began teaching classes for the unemployed here, and the question for us was what did we want to make of workers education. Was it to teach confrontation, pure and simple, or to help organize workers to take over and run this crazy system in a socially-recognized humanist way? John Dewey thought of education as the agency of communication and it was from him that we drew much of our intellectual energy.

Let me read you from a lecture I gave some 30 years ago summarizing workers education. I am attacking the textbooks and saying where they've gone wrong: "The imposing periods of the Declaration of Independence and of the Constitution are rightly known to students, but even in Massachusetts the school children are being told little about Daniel Shay and his fellow rebels, who were cheated out of the land for which they had fought to gain the British tyranny." You may recall Archibald MacLeish's lines in "Land of the Free": "Boston taught him, Boston, embalmer of history, blots his name off on the school book page." Our children are told about Barbara Frietchie's "shoot if you must this old grey head," but not about the dauntless courage of Mother Jones as she faced the soldiers in the armed camps of the mining towns. Millions of children, sons and daughters of workers, do not even know her name despite her heroism which, like that of other rebels in those company towns, was equal to that displayed at Valley Forge. It is chiefly at their own union classes that the garment workers first learn about the courage and daring of Clara Lemlich and her fellow waistmakers in 1909, and the awful tragedy of the Triangle fire in New York City in 1911.

Scant mention, if any, is given in the history books to trade unions and to men like Samuel Gompers and Eugene V. Debs. Only recently have attempts been made to rescue Tom Paine from the vile libel by which partisan religious sects besmirched his record of service to the American Revolution. Very few history books quote the speeches of Abraham Lincoln on the right to strike and on the superior claims of the man above the dollar. We have forgotten that when Horace Mann spoke about free education he said that thereby free men and women would be created. Professional patrioteering groups have tried to falsify history in order to fortify reaction.

The teachers in the American Federation of Teachers and in other progressive groups have done their best to remedy past mistakes. We have to fill up the dangerous gaps left in our learning. Workers education has its own problems. Is it just going to be an administration yes-man chorus, proving that the union leaders are the best guys ever, despite the many times their members get bored with seeing too many pictures of the same union leader in the same union journal? Is it going to be an anti-administration caucus, in which the rebels get together in order to plot? Or is there a middle caucus in which we keep open the precious rights of discussion, progressive criticism, and the right to grow? Is the teaching of workers education in the schools taking the bite out of it? Is it going to be a sort of support for the status quo? Are we going to look over some of the problems that face the mass of workers who are still unorganized in the United States and realize that workers education must go back and look at basics again?

JULIUS MANSON • I'm delighted to share this experience with Mark Starr for personal reasons that go back a long way.

He reminded me how far they go back quite unexpectedly when he said that his education began in 1907. That was when I was born. He has been on a continuous voyage. The education hasn't stopped. If there is any aspect to workers education that should be stressed, I think precisely that it is a voyage that is endless, even though Mark seems to feel that it stops by the time we raise our class. I should think that at that time we would simply change our programs and continue the educational process. And if he sounds very much like an idealist to you by suggesting that it isn't simply a matter of personal fulfillment as much as it is advancing the interests of the whole class, recall that this is practically what happened in Denmark when Denmark ended serfdom in the last century. How many of you have ever heard of an extraordinary character by the name of Nikolai Grundtvig, who started the Danish folk high school?

When we discuss workers education and its aspirations, we ought to pay some tribute to the remarkable schools that were set up mainly to help the freed Danish serfs to learn how to read, to write, and to run their farms intelligently. In my lifetime, it was possible to watch Denmark move from what was a quagmire among nations when it came to illiteracy, to being turned completely around. Workers education did it. When it was too cold to work on the farms, the sons of the farmers were sent to these folk high schools. Even the women could go to these schools, although not in the same session. Quite a change has taken place since those days, especially when we consider what happened at Hudson Shore Labor School. But before I tell you about Hudson Shore Labor School, I would like to find out how familiar you are with what Mark and I are here to talk about.

For instance, how many people are familiar with the campaigns for Congress by the socialist Meyer London on the Lower East Side? A socialist candidate being elected to the Congress of the United States is a very important chapter in American social history. And then the campaigns of Morris Hillquit, who was famous for the number of times that he wasn't elected. He ran for mayor as a socialist. When I was a child on the Lower East Side, I wanted to know more about this movement. I was just beginning to think for myself, and

I heard about the Rand School for Social Science. The Rand School didn't ask people for qualifications, didn't require them to prove whether they could read or write or even understand. The people who came there plainly weren't cabbage heads. They were interested enough to voluntarily come and listen. And the people who were invited to speak were men like Upton Sinclair, W.E.B. DuBois, Jack London, Bertrand Russell.

That should give you some notion of the scope of workers education, its context. Let me give you the name of one fellow who wasn't very well known in the beginning and then got to be known. He started at the Rand School and another institution not very far away called the Labor Lyceum, both of which were on the Lower East Side. His name is Will Durant, an absolutely magnificent speaker who didn't mind talking to anybody. And when I say anybody, I mean that even if there was only one person in the audience he would speak. But after awhile he managed to get thousands in the audience because he was attracting people who weren't so much interested in raising their class (though they were part of a group that wanted to raise their class) as that they wanted to learn things for themselves.

That tradition goes all the way back. It includes other institutions. The ILGWU's educational department is one, headed by an absolutely extraordinary woman, who preceded Mark Starr, Manya Cohen. (I thought that some day I would write her biography, but never did; fortunately someone else is doing it and is going to get a Ph.D. for it.) The kinds of classes that were provided people who worked for a living and who never believed they would have the chance to go to school anywhere were nothing short of extraordinary. The subject matter that was introduced to them included English, learning to read and write it, public speaking, American history, labor history, labor union administration. After a few years of this exciting stuff, thrilled by what they were achieving, some of these people attended evening school and got degrees, finally.

The ILGWU also used to run a series called the Officer Qualification Courses that enabled workers to qualify as candidates for union office. If you took and passed seven courses, you were eligible. The way officers in the ILGWU seemed to hold on to their posts permanently, it was unlikely that anyone else would get a chance to run for office. But the classes gave members the chance nonetheless to say yes, they were interested. And they'd have the opportunity to take on this remarkable series of courses.

Another workers' organization that I hope you've heard about, or will read about, is the Women's Trade Union League. A whole series of famous American women was connected with it; they ran classes mostly for women, and then for men and women, in their little building over on 34th Street and Lexington Avenue for years and years. They supplied a great deal of the intellectual manpower and womanpower for the strikes that were taking place at the time.

Following the example of the ILGWU experience, there was established the Summer School for Workers, which then became the Hudson Shore Labor School in West Park, New York. It was started by Hilda Wilmington Smith, who preferred to be known by the name of Jane, and who was a dean at Bryn Mawr. The school was located at West Park, which was her family's estate, virtually opposite Hyde Park where the Roosevelts lived. In fact, Eleanor Roosevelt was a member of the Board. When it became Hudson Shore Labor School, we would have people coming up from the deep South, people who had never been inside a school, textile workers, mainly black, women, men, young, middle-aged, old. Surely we had to learn the things that we couldn't get in the ordinary school system. So we learned about labor history, we learned about what could be called labor economics, we learned something about parliamentary procedure. We also had courses in what have since become known as techniques in role playing. We had projects in which everybody pitched in. I think one of the greatest tributes to the way this school operated was the sadness experienced every time a class ended. The people who had to go back home had had a chance to live as civilized human beings. It was a total experience, not just instruction alone.

Hudson Shore continued for a good long time in its irreverent fashion, but it could not get adequate support from the American labor movement. It was supported by particular organizations, local or international—the UAW or the IUE might say, "Let's pay for a two-week or a three-week course in shop steward training"—but that was too occasional. The most important thing that the Hudson Shore Labor School did was allow people to see what was possible for them to learn in this world through courses in art, philosophy, history, music. That went on for 20 years and then vanished.

As a result of the interest that developed in these classes— which were designed exclusively for the purpose of workers education—there were people who wanted to continue their studies. They wanted to get college degrees. Indeed, some wanted to teach, ultimately. So in 1947, with the labor movement's backing, New York State established the School of Industrial Labor Relations at Cornell. One of the school's early achievements, by the way, was compiling for the first time a history of the labor movement for use in high schools. We couldn't get a commercial publisher to produce it, but the State paid for publication, and it has been used widely by high schools. In any case, people began to take the courses at the School of Industrial Relations, many of them coming from the labor movement. The trouble was that when they graduated, they couldn't get jobs in the labor movement. They went off into management instead, and the labor movement became a bit cross with Cornell. It now has decided to do something else. We have a new institution in the State, called Empire State College, with one location in New York City. Empire State College is theoretically education without walls, where those persons coming from industry, especially those working for a living and who haven't had a chance to go beyond the minimal educational levels, can be motivated to move along into the so-called higher levels of education. For those people who had the will to go beyond workers education and get into formal education, the path was available.

I'd like to make another point apropos of this. This whole idea of education, it is not generally known, has very deep roots in the labor movement. In this country, for example, when union people normally had their day in court it was as defendants. They were allowed no other role for a long while; as a member of a union you were a member of a criminal conspiracy. You had to do something else. So some of them formed educational societies. And they set up things that had fancy names, like Labor Lyceum. These Labor Lyceums were used by the infant—not infantile—but infant labor unions for the purposes of having their people learn what made this world the way it was. In the 1820's, they formed the first workingmen's parties. And what was one of the most important central planks in the platform of these parties? Free education. In fact, Horace Mann is connected to that early labor experience of workingmen's parties, which called for public education. If it weren't for that impulse, we'd have delayed the whole concept of public education for generations.

You've both talked about the different subject matter in the labor education schools and how their curriculums differed from the regular schools. Could you talk a little bit about the differences in pedagogy or style in the labor school as opposed to the regular school, if there were any?

STARR ● I think we worked within the tradition associated now with open education. It's quite difficult when you have 40 adult students to have a conversation for an hour and 30 minutes. So you pull the table off the podium and put the chairs round in a circle and tell everybody not to let any statement pass by that (1) they don't understand or (2) they disagree with. That's what we did. Moreover, we were dealing with mature students, the most intelligent, active, mentally alert groups in the movement. I think we were using what might be called progressive education methods, as far as methods of instruction go. But for the rest, I think a lot of our people were good teachers almost by instinct. Sometimes the earlier classes weren't so good because the teacher was learning at the expense of his student. That takes place in public education, too, of course. Some of our best teachers were apprentices without college degrees or things of that sort, but they learned how to hold interest, how to keep the discussion going. I would think that the best that you have

* NOTE: Direct questions from the audience are interspersed through these and other reminiscences, and appear in italics.

developed in your open school movement was anticipated in part and in practice by workers education activities.

MANSON • I don't believe there is much of a difference between the teaching methods of workers education and regular education. It depends on the teacher, the students, the atmosphere, the circumstances. There is one difference, however, that I think restricts the teacher in the formal educational atmosphere as distinguished from one in the workers educational atmosphere. That's the requirement to follow an outline rigorously and to evaluate students by giving them grades. I happen to favor grades when you want a degree. I'm opposed to them if you don't need a degree. These people are not taking courses for credit. They're doing it voluntarily. Every one of them comes in already motivated. All of them are mature. It's a marvelous reservoir to tap. You discover extraordinary talent in groups like that. For that reason, the class knows you're not taking advantage of them by seemingly talking about something not in the outline. They know that when you do that it's going to illuminate a point that someone else might have raised in class.

Moreover, in workers education you can take time to repeat something that is not clear to somebody. You don't have to rush to finish up the outline. If someone raises a question that may not be clear to the rest of the class, you try to show the connection. In the process, it becomes clearer even to the student who raised the point in the first place. In the formal situation, you don't have time for that. You're not going to see the class very much. Again, if it was a Hudson Shore situation, why you don't stop teaching at any hour of the day. You're with the people all of the time and they raise questions and they get into discussions. As a matter of fact, one of the most heartening aspects of workers education and the Hudson Shore atmosphere was the constant bull session we had, running into all hours of the morning or the night.

STARR • There was a cultural aspect to workers education too. It wasn't necessary to take a deliberate class angle on everything. We always said that the people coming up from below weren't confronting reality if they didn't examine every corner of the literature. Indeed, that meant literature. The experience of working for your living, and the experience of seeing exploitation and rebelling against it, the experience of winning a voice about conditions in the shop where previously you were afraid to voice them, that should be and is expressed in poetry and in literature. I don't think the concentration must be on social science.

There is just tons of stuff around about what the WPA did. The students ran into the hundreds of thousands who would never have achieved their diplomas otherwise. There are unions that do their own work directly because they don't trust the professors and they run their own programs. There are other unions that very definitely work in conjunction with the state universities. There's a whole union organization, Local 189, comprised of teachers in workers education. The membership is nationwide. Mr. Shanker thinks we're a blue sky local. To some extent, that's true. We get out our own listing and directory of colleges that maintain industrial relations classes. In the main, the classes are in collective bargaining and job evaluation, as well as some in general theory, history, economics, and things of that sort.

Every union does its own thing. Julius mentioned ILGWU's Officer Qualification Courses. We tried there to keep open the avenues of criticism. I think those courses were the best, most cultural kind of leavening that the locals ever had. There are men and women in office at the ILGWU today who, I think, are better persons for having been exposed to the questions those classes asked: What was the ILGWU? What was the ILGWU's relation to the labor movement? What was the labor movement doing as a whole? We had classes in parliamentary law because, after all, you have to learn those things to be practical in trade union conferences and meetings. There were classes in public speaking because you have to organize your thoughts as you organized your fellow members. But, in the main, workers education focused on getting the organizer who was out in some tough struggle to come in and tell his experience. The classes were drawn from life: how to keep trade union books, how to keep people honest, how to avoid getting their finances all mixed up with what is known as pocket financing—putting something in one pocket and something in the other and then wondering why the union accounts are in a mess. I know this sounds very small, but it was important to the clear, progressive, decent operation of the union.

Background Playground in Nurses Settlement, Henry Street. Late 1890s. Photo by Jacob Riis. Library of Congress.

Free night school for immigrants in a New York public school. No date. Library of Congress.

Settlement Houses

... you get to know the people so well that they'll work with you on the changing of the social conditions, which are so bad.

HELEN HALL • I'll begin by telling you some of the reasons why I think the settlement house is useful, what it represents. It stands for a group of people in a neighborhood seeking to identify the problems of that neighborhood and seeking to bring to the neighborhood some of the answers to the problems. This is the basic thing. I've stayed in it all these years because I found it so utterly rewarding to work for and with the people that I was there to help. I knew my neighbors, I knew the children, I knew the teenagers, I knew the adults, I knew the old people. I knew them personally. They were friends.

I had a lovely experience the other day. About two weeks ago, one of the older women from Henry Street telephoned me and said she'd like to talk to me just for a little while and where could she do it. We settled on Henry Street as the place. A few others, who'd been heads of groups at the settlement house, joined us; there were about 10 or so, and we sat for two of the nicest hours I ever spent. They all talked practically at once and told me about the things they'd learned at Henry Street that they'd taken into their own communities. They no longer lived on the Lower East Side. But they'd started the same thing over where they now lived. And one woman said, "Do you remember when you saved my boy by helping him get his degree?" Well, I didn't remember. But anyway, it's nice that she did. Another one said, "You know, Miss Hall, we knew you were the leader all right, but you were always one of us."

That's what you try to do. You are there presumably because you have certain skills to apply to changing conditions and in getting people to work with you on it. But it's not always easy to work with them. I mean it's not easy. And I loved it. One of the last things I did when I left Henry Street was a big job getting petitions signed for Gouverneur Hospital, which is a little hospital we fought to save, while everybody tried to kill it. In the neighborhood, you just mentioned Gouverneur and people told you in one breath how bad it was—"but we've got to have it." We fought for years—one thing that all the neighbors did no matter whether they were black, white, Puerto Rican, or Jewish—we all got together to fight for Gouverneur. We collected 34,000 signatures to give them to the Borough President. It was one of the actions that helped save that hospital. And that, I think, is what the settlement house represents.

The idea of the settlement house comes through all the things you do—the clubs, the athletics, the music, the dance—all the things that you bring into the neighborhood. Through them, you get to know the people so well that they'll work with you on the changing of the social conditions, which are so bad. That's what you want. You want them to be working with you. You get to know them through the various things you're working with. I don't need to tell you that human beings need some kind of artistic expression. The settlements try to bring the best there is in music and dance and painting and all the other things that enrich the lives of the children and the adults and the old people there. In the process, you get to know what people need and you get them to know what they should do, too. Because, after all, this is a job that you do with them.

During Mayor LaGuardia's time, we organized a big procession to City Hall to protest the high price of milk. We were trying to get the attention of the Governor. This is what we did to get attention: We decided to bring a cow to City Hall. We had been trying to establish a milk cooperative that would keep the price of milk down. I don't mean to go into all the details, but we had a hard time getting a license for it. I won't go into all our enemies in this world because there were quite a few we worked against. In any case, it was raining and awful. We'd asked mothers to bring baby carriages, and we brought one cow along. We eventually got the license. It enabled the milk cooperative to deal directly with the farmer and the consumer. Then the mothers of the neighborhood who got involved in all this went around to the stores to make them buy our milk. So it is the kind of thing that you just do day in and day out because the problems that are facing you are food and clothing and jobs. Those things are the things you fought about.

I remember when I first went to Henry Street, walking up and down the tenement stairs and thinking as I walked, "I'll get rid of these houses or I'll die." You know, really, they were so ugly, so filthy. The children had to live in the midst of that. It's seeing it yourself that makes it different. It's one of the reasons I've stayed in the settlements all these years. It's because the thing I was going to take to the President, let us say, was something I knew myself; I saw it. And I was met on the corner every minute by people who had a story to tell me of something that was going wrong.

During one period, we had to fight against gang warfare, which involved gangs that were pretty fierce and pretty hard and rough. One of my associates at Henry Street had observed the gangs and had understood how each gang grew. Each had a little predelinquent gang, a bunch of boys, past 10, 11 and so forth, who decided to imitate the older boys in the gang. Say the gang was called "The Lords," the younger boys would call themselves "The Young Lords" and take on all the attributes of The Lords—follow them, watch them, and hang on the outskirts to see how they could be as much like The Lords as possible. So my associate said, "I'm going to get the parents involved." Now, I don't know whether you know it but it's very hard when kids are gang age—16, 17, 18, 19—to get their parents to work with you. By then the parents have lost their hold. But the parents haven't lost their hold with the 10-year-old or 11-year-old or 12-year-old. So what we did was to take whoever the children were, with the names taken mostly from The Lords, and get the families to meet with us. We said, "We will help keep your kids out of the gang warfare if you will work with us at every point. Everytime they do anything wrong you will have to come." We were building a relationship between the child and the parent that we thought might keep them straight. Well, it worked so well that the settlements all over the city got a good grant to continue and expand the project. And it really worked. No matter what little thing they did wrong, we sent for the parents and we all talked it over. It was a matter of supporting the authority of the family. It was a situation that worked.

These are the kinds of things you see in your neighborhood and you think of ways of treating them and the neighbors work with you on it, the parents work and are awfully interested in this.

I'd like to just tell how we got our Mental Hygiene Clinic started. It was long, long ago. And we had a little kid, eight years old, who went absolutely mad every time we closed the afternoon program. She bit, scratched, and screamed, and wouldn't go out. Well, we realized there was something psychologically wrong there; she needed help. So I called the hospitals, I called everything in the city that I could think of, and I couldn't get help for her for six months. It was six months before that child could get any help or I could get her into a psychiatric clinic. I decided we'd better bring in a psychiatrist and do it ourselves. And that was the beginning. We raised money immediately for the psychiatric care of the girl.

But this is how it goes. This is how this close relationship between the neighbors and the problems of the neighborhood and your effort to provide the cultural things builds life. It's all part of the same process.

As part of this, we tried to bring into the neighborhood teachers who were not only beautiful and skillful people, but who also cared about other people. It wasn't just the art we wanted to develop, it was also the person. I remember a boy who loved to work as a potter; he loved making pottery. But his father thought he was wasting time. The son was about 11 or 12, and family disapproval is an awful burden to a kid. Fortunately his teacher realized that the boy wasn't really getting where he ought to on his pottery because of the feelings generated by his father's nagging. So she put one of the boy's pots, or whatever he was making, in an art exhibition room, and turned on all the lights, and then got the father to come. He was so pleased by the fact that his boy could make anything that she would exhibit, and put a light on it, that he dropped his disapproval, for the time being anyway. This is what I mean when I say we have to have teachers who not only can teach a boy pottery but who can understand him well enough to go to his family and get his family to appreciate it, too.

H. DANIEL CARPENTER • Let me preface this by saying when I walked down the hall here and saw the session on the one-room country school, I was tempted to go in because the first six years of my schooling were spent in a one-room country school, and it was one of the great experiences of my life. Let me come back to the subject historically. I mean, for some of us who have been interested in education, you can't be interested in people or neighborhoods and families without having a historical perspective. I think somebody here mentioned the fact that her mother attended English classes in the settlements. You can almost trace the history of immigration by looking at films of the people who came to the classes. The settlement house reached out to those coming to our land. Anyone who needed help in English could get it by studying in one of the settlement classes. These were established, I think, prior to the ones established by the Board of Education. And the program continues, even while the city is taking steps to try to end theirs.

First the kindergartens, then the nurseries, then day care, then Head Start—all of these found a home in the settlement house. In more recent years, the mini-schools have been started there, as well as the tutoring programs that try to help or motivate youngsters to take advantage of what schools can give. The whole field of progressive education, I think, distinguished itself in settlement work, particularly in what we call group work. We used many of the ideas and practices of child development and child-centered programs in working with the children and with the groups themselves, so there was quite an overlap. We've been interested in providing classes for Civil Service exams and developing all kinds of skills. Many of the skills that we set up and that people acquired, became vocational skills, as well. People began to earn a living from what they'd learned at the settlements. The interest in helping people acquire skills is one of the things I want to talk about in a little bit more detail.

Back in 1908, down on the West Side, where the Hudson Guild was located at the time, there was a big printing industry. But the young people who came to Hudson Guild couldn't get into printing; they couldn't get the skills in school. So our director decided that maybe the Guild should start a school of printing. We found a very good printer, bought some equipment, and started giving practice classes in setting type. And before long the school was very popular. Something like 30 or 40 young people were in it, and in 1910 they graduated a class. But then none of them could get work because they didn't belong to the union. So there was a good deal of discussion about this; we held talks with industry and with the union, and finally both the industry and the union, along with the Hudson Guild, decided to co-sponsor the school, which became the New York School for Printers Apprentices. From 1911 to 1918, it was operated by the three groups. After 1938, coming up to the end of the Depression, with things still tough, they brought the Board of Education into it also, and the school became the New York High School for Printing. That arrangement set the pattern for starting vocational schools from that point on. For example, the High School of Fashion Industries developed out of a meeting between the union and the garment industry. And so on. We're rather pleased with having made that kind of contribution as far as education is concerned. Because of our interest, the curriculum came to include economics and labor education—a more humanistic approach than previously the case. The high school also provides now not only for the apprentices—a clause which, by the way, is built into contracts between the printing industry and the unions—it's now a retraining school for journeymen, a need that exists because the printing industry has changed so from what it was years ago. I think its graduates have influenced the printing industry throughout the world.

I'm wondering what you did as educators or social workers in a situation where there was a conflict on philosophy. For example, in Chelsea, on Ninth Avenue and 28th Street, where my father had a little delicatessen and I worked as a teenager, I knew that the families were sort of authoritarian and old world. They weren't particularly receptive to progressive education, especially in dealing with kids, where there would be a democratic interaction. How did you bridge the gap, if in fact there was one? Was there a conflict in philosophy between what you tried to do in the nursery school and what the child really practiced and saw in the family?

CARPENTER ● In the 1930s, we had a long waiting list of people for places in kindergarten. I went around looking for about a half dozen mothers who would be willing to help start a cooperative and share the running of things. After awhile, we finally got some people interested. We got a teacher who would work and parents who would come in and sort of help as well as they could. I think we often kidded ourselves; you know, people worked hard when everybody was looking and so forth, and when no one was there—whack—that's all. But I think that this was one of the ways of building into people's minds that there is another way besides the way they're accustomed to. Of course, it didn't always work. Some families hold much tighter standards of conduct. I remember one man saying, "Well, I asked my daughter where she had been, and she said, 'It's really none of your business, Pop,' so I slapped her and, you know, she rolled down bawling; she never said that to me again." Now this is exactly what you're talking about when you raised that question. The only thing to do with that situation is work at it.

HALL ● I think that's the thing—you work at it. I mean it's so important that you have all sorts of devices where people meet. They meet in clubs and groups, and they meet in art, in the art schools; you devise ways where they meet together and talk things over and get to know each other. It's not easy, particularly when you get a change of population in a neighborhood. The people who have always lived there resent the new people. You, in the settlement house, have to set that example there. Drawing together the new and the old is one of the most serious problems that the settlement faces. We're not always successful, but sometimes we are.

One of the times, when we were getting a lot of new people in, we turned our girls' camp into a day camp and took people there from the neighborhood in buses, three or four buses, every day. The newcomers and the oldtimers went in the same buses and sang each other's songs. When they came back home, they were friendly. They'd eaten together, and they'd gone swimming together, and they'd done a lot of things together that they hadn't done in the neighborhood. This was one thing we did directly with the idea of getting the new and old neighbors together.

We were largely Jewish in that neighborhood, with a scattering of Italians. And then blacks and Puerto Ricans came in. It was a mixture. But as the new people came in, we tried to think of ways to have them just roam together automatically, not for any reason at all, but to go to camp and have a good day. And they took the whole family, as a matter of fact; we did family camping. It was a very successful way of drawing new neighbors together.

CARPENTER ● We drew staff from everywhere. Wherever we could find the best people. We deliberately avoided taking everybody from either outside or inside the neighborhood. We thought mixture would be the important thing. In the 1950s and 1960s we were sometimes caught up in a series of arguments by people holding that "you got to take from the neighborhood." Somehow people feel if you live in the neighborhood you have, in some sense, extra ability or skill, which isn't true. And we deliberately avoided this.

HALL ● Was there any communication between the public school and the settlements? Well, I was on the school board. Not the present school board, but the old school board that had very little power. But you did learn a lot and you got to know all the principals around you and their possibilities and impossibilities. I think we had to be close with the schools if we were doing a good job in the neighborhood. Once we had to work out an arrangement with the schools about eight children who were having some difficulty. They weren't backward mentally—they were eight years old—but they weren't manageable in the school and they weren't sent to an institution, they were just out in the streets. So working through the Mental Hygiene Clinic, we provided psychiatric counseling—we did it for three years—and seven out of the eight were able to go back to school and function there. These things you do as experiments, hoping that it will be used, if you prove that they're good.

CARPENTER ● In the last 10 years that I was at Hudson Guild, we did a number of things. One was we had all the principals come in for lunch with our staff. And then sometimes we'd get invited to one school or another. Sometimes we'd get things going all year long and about once a month we'd get together. One of the school principals was on the board of the Guild. And then, most ambitious of all, we collaborated with the school nearest to us, P.S. 33, in the late 1950s and early 1960s on a closed circuit television program, which we broadcast between P.S. 33 and 600 units of housing at the Hudson Guild and the Health Centers. We had great dreams about this. It was something that you seldom got. It involved collaborating with the Housing Authority as well as the school. We made an effort to stay in very close contact with the principals of the schools, as well as with the mental health programs and the tutoring programs, such as College Bound, with our neighborhood community conferences, with city health services, with everything. You have to work at it. There were some principals, I remember over the years, who weren't too happy about collaborating and others who were most happy with it. It was one of the very happy things that, as Helen said, gave you reason to stay in this work. People who cared and really worked together. It was one of the reasons I stayed in it.

The *Shule*

. . . we learned for the love of the experience. I do not remember if there were grades and report cards. Possibly there were, but they must have been very unimportant if they were used. Our teachers were people with authority, but in the best sense of their loving and caring for us, openly and unabashedly . . .

LOUIS COHEN • The time I'm talking about is roughly from 1916 to 1921, from my tenth to my fifteenth year. I was born and grew up on the Lower East Side of New York, with brief excursions to other parts of the city. The Lower East Side in those days was dense with people, more so than today, and almost all of them were Yiddish-speaking and East European Jewish and first-generation Americans. It was an interesting population, much more so, I think, than its largely middle-class, homogenized, and conformist descendant group. Dynamic and vibrant, undergoing social, economic, political, and ideological change of explosive intensity, it was caught up in making the swift transition from the orthodox life of centuries to new forms of relating to life, to society, to daily problems. While orthodoxy—bearded, introverted, dreamily engrossed in God and in ongoing conversation with Him which was worship—was alive and well, and synagogues big and little were everywhere, as were the religious day schools we call *yeshivas* and the afterschool religious schools known as *talmud torahs,* secularism also flourished. Some of it was intellectual and unpolitical; I would associate the name of Morris R. Cohen with this aspect of Lower East Side life. But most of this secularism, except for the Zionists, designated itself as radical. Some of that was anarchist, most of it socialist; there was also a national-socialist movement known as Poale

Zion or worker-Zionist. These movements were comprised of the Jewish working class of the city, the immigrant men and women who worked—toiled is the better word—in the sweatshops of those days, and who were caught up in the tragic and heroic trade union struggles of the time. The needle trades unions and some others grew out of these struggles.

These left-wing, often avowedly revolutionary, movements were only one wing of the dynamic thrust into political modernism of this young immigrant population. The other was nationalist, that is, Zionist, with its aspiration toward the establishment of a Jewish state in Palestine as the solution to what we used to call the Jewish problem. The leadership of this movement was largely middle class and, it seemed to me then, external to the vibrant working class life of the community. But its left wing, the Poale Zion, to which I have referred, was very much a part of that life, and it tried to fuse the best of both the national and the working class movements: the *folk* aspiration that grew out of being Jewish and suffering oppression because we were Jewish, and the *class* orientation, the dream of socialism, which offered *its* solutions to mass poverty and oppression.

This movement, as did every trend among the immigrant Jewish population, rode on a remarkable floodtide of Yiddish literary, journalistic, and theatrical activity, whose vigor and variety of outlook would startle us today. Both national-cultural and working class in orientation, the Poale Zion at that time placed its emphasis on Yiddish rather than Hebrew. For Yiddish, they said then, was the language of the great majority of the Jewish masses.

The Poale Zion founded a fraternal organization, the Jewish National Workers Alliance, its counterpart to the socialist and at the time, nonnationalist, Workmens Circle. The Alliance, or Farband, in turn, established a new type of school for children: the *folkshule*, or nonreligious, national, more accurately, folk-cultural and socialist-minded children's school. Its curriculum consisted of Yiddish language, Yiddish literature, Jewish song, Jewish history, Jewish holidays, Jewish life. (Ambitiously, the *shule* I went to also taught us Hebrew, with moderate success.) These Farband *shules* (for they branched out throughout the city and the continent) were the first of their kind. After World War I, other groups of *shules* arose, with differing political (or nonpolitical) orientations, but all of them equally absorbed in the life of Yiddish-speaking Jews and their literature. The Farband *shules* were either Saturday-Sunday schools or afternoon schools meeting on Mondays to Thursdays and on Sunday mornings. It was to one such, in Harlem, where we lived briefly, that my parents took me. I dragged my feet going, but I was won over almost the minute I got there. The following fall, when we moved back to the Lower East Side, I entered the *shule* there, and that was where I had my wonderful learning and loving experience for a number of years.

What was it that won my heart and my imagination so strongly, as it did those of so many other children, and carried me there day after day for years? I think, first of all, it was that the young men who taught us—the teachers were all men in that particular school—took delight in us, saw in us the human beauty, the lyricism that they felt in themselves. How many of them were aware of the educational idealism of Froebel, Pestalozzi, and the progressive educators of the time in America I do not know, but they certainly were of that cast.

Secondly, I think it had to do with the fact that they loved the subject matter of their curriculum, in particular the body of Yiddish literature, and won our love for it, seemingly effortlessly. This is not surprising. Yiddish writing, like its Irish counterpart of the same period, dealt with ordinary folk who were caught in the toils of poverty, oppression, and degradation and who stood up to their fate with endurance, with protest (to God often as not), with humor, and with loyalty to those they loved. As to the language of the literature that was being opened to us, Yiddish was our mother tongue even though we spoke English more readily, and the literature was about our people, ourselves. Aspiration, the new, the romantic and adventurous are important to children, but so are roots, and here they were for us, in this language, this literature, this life, all familiar and intimate, yet all taking on forms of beauty. Our teachers spread these before us copiously and with joy.

So roots in forms of beauty were the third reason the school held us. Perhaps this is the moment for me to digress briefly and talk about my simultaneous education in the public schools, where, of course, I was made aware of American and British cultural values and the literature of the English language. I was responsive to that too, to *Evangeline* and *Miles Standish,* to *Abou ben Adhem* and *Julius Caesar,* but not with the same total enlistment of feeling, for these impersonations of human experience were, if not strangers, at any rate familiars once removed and somewhat abstract for me, as Sholem Aleichem's and Peretz's characters were not. For me, in late childhood and early adolescence, the latter were my gateway to humanity beyond ethnicity and borders, as the former could not yet quite be.

Speaking of the public school brings me, by way of contrast, to a fourth reason for the magic of the *shule* for me. For not only was the subject matter of the public school too remote, the way it was taught was impersonal: the teachers were themselves distant. The classroom atmosphere was cold, the discipline strict and imposed, and teaching was punishing even when it was interesting. That is, there was always a mark, a grade at the end of the road, compiled from marks earned several times each day and from tests every Friday. So dominant was this aspect of public education that any grade below the highest few was a disappointment, a letdown, a blow to one's ego. And, of course, such learning was intensely competitive. It wasn't that as a bright young pupil you wanted to shine; it was that you wanted to *outshine* the other bright young ones—a distortion, in my view, of the learning process. In sum, the public school was not only cold and punitive, its spirit was combative like the jousting of knights; individuality was discouraged and stunted and at the same time emulatively aroused. This was true even when your teacher was interesting and the disciplined classroom milieu comfortable.

This combative spirit stood in marked contrast to the atmosphere of learning in the *shule,* where we learned for the love of the experience. I do not remember if there were grades and report cards. Possibly there were, but they must have been very unimportant if they were used. Our teachers were people of authority, but in the best sense of their loving and caring for us, openly and unabashedly, of trusting and respecting us—we were completely at ease with them—and of their being sources of beauty and enlightenment for us. So this, the atmosphere of happy learning, was the fourth reason for the magic of the *shule*.

There was a fifth positive aspect to the *shule* life—its invitation, at all available hours, to come through its open door, to belong there, to develop activities of our own in an atmosphere of total acceptance, of freedom to just be there, to just move about within its walls. For me, it wasn't just being able to play handball, which I did, avidly, in the backyard of our little building. We developed literary clubs, a drama group, a dance club, all of which met on Saturdays. They were our own, our creation, and they were very active.

As I said, the atmosphere was welcoming and free inside as well as outside of class. We were a disciplined group; ours was a total response in attitude to the attitude we felt toward us (I do not remember any enforcement, scolding, or reproach by the staff). We were disciplined because we loved what we came for. When we went to classes each day, we were content, courteous, and quiet while our teachers led our discussions and taught us.

Lingering at the *shule* was part of the happiness of the place. I do not remember ever wanting to linger at the public school, let alone return to it for after-school activities, though some did for the athletics, which were, of course, competitive. There did not seem to be anyone there who cared for me, or for any of us. To be fair, there must have been some, at least, among the teachers who did, but the mode of discipline and teaching was such that it didn't come through. My guess is that it had to do with something that underlay that mode and distanced the public school experience for children—and that was the purpose of the kind of education we were receiving. We were being molded, carved, chiseled—and, in the process, inadequately fed spiritually—toward an end that did not suit our needs, the end being for us to become pliable and controllable employees and citizens with adequate skills, rather than autonomous, self-propelled, thinking, resourceful, loving, social, and constantly growing human beings who worked, of course, and were citizens too, but who knew what we were about and functioned accordingly.

There was something else still. This *shule* was an "open" school, as you may have surmised by now. As such, it was open to the parents as well, and because we were happy there, our parents came and participated in its life, and this served to reinforce the meaningfulness of the experience for us. As you know, parents of public school children are not encouraged to come and participate in the life of the school, even when they are invited *pro forma*. The atmosphere is authoritarian and cold. The schools are not open, not very inviting. At least in our big cities and industrial towns they are not, generally, though I would guess that some are happier places today.

Let me mention still another facet of my *shule* experience. I spoke of roots a while ago, roots in folk life and in the people who toil and struggle, which the *shule* nurtured in us. There were roots of another kind, now in deep neglect, of which those wonderful young men who taught us were aware: roots in nature, the green world of summer. Where we lived and went to school, both schools, there was literally not a tree for blocks around, nor any grass except the most furtive and unappetizing blades that grew between the pavement cracks. And so, during the long summer vacations, on every Wednesday, we were taken for long days of picnicking to verdant, sun-drenched grounds in either Bronx Park or Van Cortlandt Park. Our parents went too when they could. These were for me lyrical experiences, unforgettable and everlastingly enriching.

Why did it not occur to our public school people that we needed such experiences as we needed water?

Let me conclude with a personal confession. Those years are very distant from my life today. English is the language I live by, almost totally. My Yiddish, idiosyncratic and vivid, has fallen into a state of considerable desuetude, I am sorry to say, though its idiom springs forward to serve me not infrequently. And I am international in my interests. That is, my loyalties and my loves go out to all the world, though I continue to have an abiding concern for the fate of my own people. But I doubt that I would have been as richly empathic for all who toil and suffer and languish and struggle and aspire under our common sun had I not been nurtured as I was in that Lower East Side *shule*.

At the same time, I think that because of that experience, I understand better what actuates this country's most economically depressed ethnic groups, the blacks, the Puerto Ricans, the Mexican-Americans, the Indians. As far as education is concerned, one part of their demand is simple enough: Teach our children adequately so they can better cope. That demand has to do with skills, particularly reading. But the parents of the children of these minorities want something else too, I think. They want their children recognized as persons, enjoyed as they enjoy them, and loved. Such recognition includes their right to their cultural values: their songs, literature, history, yes, even their language, their mother tongue, *in the schools they attend*. Bringing these in and articulating them in our classrooms—again, with regard and love—would go far to winning the hearts and minds—if I may use this abused term—of these young people to the wonderful, joyous adventure of becoming learners. And it means bringing their parents in as participants in the daily life and ongoing learning of the schools their children attend.

This kind of openness goes for all our teachers, our children, and their parents, but it goes double for our ethnic minorities. For what, after all, is open education? It is much more than the opening up of classroom space and extending it to several rooms and the corridors alongside them. It is, for teachers, opening their sensibilities and their minds to the children, for the children, opening their minds and imaginations and partisanships to the world, for the school, opening its doors to the parents as cooperators and learners. In all, it is loving and learning, learning and loving.

This was the *shùle* for me, and, for me at least, its lesson for our time.

Developing a New Educational Agenda

DAVID HAWKINS • In honor of this occasion, and out of my own sense of obligation as a member of the philosophic trade, I would like today to go back into the history of our concerns and rescue from near oblivion something of the thinking of Susan Blow, whose writing I knew, in a sense, earlier than any other, including not only the "Dick and Jane" of my first-grade memories but also the English nursery rhymes and stories which I still associate with the blue sky or howling desert, as my New England mother always called it, of a West Texas early childhood. I have concrete evidence of the precocity of my own concern with the philosophy of education in four volumes from the pen of that lady, arch-exponent of the theory and practice of Friedrich Froebel. In one of those volumes there are five pages which my mother carefully pasted together again after I had worked on them a careful critical commentary, practicing the use of one of the early analytical tools of the Froebel kindergarten, a pair of blunt-nosed scissors.

To tell the truth, I have never reread those volumes until recently. And I now have a somewhat more complex reaction to them than I did as a three-year-old. On the positive side, this reaction is affected by the fact that Susan Blow was my mother's own kindergarten teacher in the St. Louis of the 1870s. Susan Blow, or Miss Susie, as she was called, was a vastly learned lady, a protege of William T. Harris, who was United States Commissioner of Education in 1894, and creator of the *Journal of Speculative Philosophy*. It was, I suppose, from this learned background that Miss Susie introduced her children to a number of items which were not in the standard Froebelian curriculum, or not as far as I know.

For example, as a young child, I heard about the tetrahedron, the octahedron, the icosahedron, and, loveliest of all, the pentagonal dodecahedron: marvelous words, forms, and names that my mother still remembered and enjoyed from her early childhood.

To give you one more slant on that 100-years-ago experience, which I shared at secondhand, I quote from Harris's own introduction to Miss Blow's book, *Symbolic Education:* "According to reports," he says, "there are in 1873"—the year I think my mother entered that kindergarten—"so far as could be learned, 42 kindergartens in the United States, with 73 teachers, and 1,252 pupils. Five years later," he says, "these had increased to 159 kindergartens, 376 teachers, and 4,797 pupils." At the time he wrote, in 1891, Harris estimated the number of kindergartens at 3,000, teachers at 5,000, pupils at 100,000. So in 20 years, the number of kindergartens had increased 30-fold, and the average class size had increased by 50 percent. Miss Susie was one of the first in this movement; she typified the movement at its best, I think. A strong practitioner, who influenced profoundly the lives of some of her children; a theorist who not only read but reflected deeply on her own practical experience. Time and again this practical acquaintance with the real world of childhood peeps out through her otherwise rather exalted prose. You can see this, for example, in her discussion of the concern she brought her children to exercise in the daily care and observation of plants and animals in her kindergarten. It puts to shame the casual window pots and the sad neglected gerbils that one finds in so many classrooms today. My mother's addiction to the garden seems also to have started at that source. Still, the prose style and the content of Susan Blow's work often required, on my part at least, an effort of historical imagination.

The style, as I said, was exalted, but never really sentimental. One can read it for substance. The hard part is, for me, in the substance. By way of background, I should remind you that the strongest influence on Froebel was the commitment, the life, the work of Pestalozzi. But the chords that were excited in Froebel by this experience were those of Hegelian idealism, and that also was the background of William T.

Harris, resonating as well with Emerson's transcendentalism. In the background also lay the great and feverish mind of Jean-Jacques Rousseau, who in turn influenced Pestalozzi and so much else in our world besides. The Hegelianism one meets here is of what we in the trade call the right-wing variety—which isn't a political term, although it may sometimes correspond with one—a Hegelianism diluted, in particular, by the preoccupations and perspectives of what I can only call genteel America. Thus, the social question was not visible in Miss Susie's writing. The emphasis was on the idealism of spirit—on the great moving spirit of history—Hegel's *Geist*. There is no trace in it of the harder and darker side of Hegel's dialectic, the side of Hegel that one can, jokingly, refer to by saying that it represents the influence on Hegel of Karl Marx. This side of Hegel, which is of great importance in the modern world, is missing.

In that latter context genteel America was, as it were, a sort of pocket of prehistory. Socialism, even in its prerevolutionary innocence, was virtually unknown. In fact, the first academic seminar in the United States on Marx's *Das Kapital* took place probably a decade later than 1892, taught at the University of Chicago by Thorstein Veblen. The philosophy of Hegel was, par excellence, the philosophy of history, a philosophy of development. If you were a student of philosophy, but had not yet come across Hegel, you were supposed to ask whether this, or that, or the other philosophical point of view was right or wrong. But when you got to Hegel, the question wasn't whether a point of view was right or wrong, because every particular philosophical point of view was ultimately going to prove wrong, but what perspective was also going to have some place in the developmental total, in the developmental whole. So you didn't have to cast out something—you simply had to find out where its limitations were and where it should be incorporated in some larger system. That's the essence of Hegel's so-called dialectic. Because it was the kind of philosophy it was, it provided a framework far more adequate than any that had come along before for the study of child development.

In a sense, I suppose, Rousseau is the inventor or at least the popularizer of the very idea of child development, but

Rousseau had a great struggle around the question of development as the expression of some inner individual hidden talent. As he saw it, and probably most correctly in the 18th century, the 'natural' development of a child, as it expressed itself genuinely, was bound to be in conflict with the world of civilization outside. Miss Susie, in her book, referred to Rousseau as an atomist. That is to say, she felt he could not see the human individual as a genuine and significant part of the larger whole. I don't think that's true of Rousseau—he wouldn't be a great philosopher if it were. But that description certainly does fit a lot of his agitated thinking. At any rate, out of this framework that she inherited from Froebel—and from Hegel and others, this Hegelian scheme of things, this spiritualistic, idealistic Hegelianism—Miss Susie selected for emphasis two basic ideas. One of these, with which Froebel is always identified, was the concept of self-activity, *Selbststätigkeit.* The other, in Froebel's language, was *Gliedganzes:* it translates roughly into "a whole that develops because it is, in turn, a part of a larger whole." It is a part whole, a participant whole.

As did Dewey, who in early life was himself a sort of middle Hegelian, neither of the right nor the left, Miss Blow emphasized that from the beginning children's learning is essentially social. She emphasized its character as a kind of human apprenticeship: an apprenticeship to the human condition. For her, children are understudies in the drama of history. They must learn their lines well before they can, as indeed they properly should, rewrite those lines themselves. Development, in her view, is an active interplay between the inner and the outer—the inner and the outer equally valued. Development is always this sort of joint fruit, never just the expression of the inner or just the assimilation of the outer. To emphasize this even further, I cannot resist quoting a passage from Blow's fascinating essay on the meaning of play, which long has been a central idea in what we call progressive education. In this passage, Miss Susie in turn quotes from a psychologist little known in our day, William Preiner of Jena:

> Having discovered the procreant idea of the kindergarten games [this is Froebel, of course] let us now endeavor to trace the gene-

Developing a New Educational Agenda

sis of the Gifts and the Occupations [all this Froebelian apparatus]. Directing our attention once again to the spontaneous deeds of childhood, we observe that the primitive impulses to express the inner and investigate the outer life manifest themselves in forms other than those thus far considered. Professor Preiner observes that "the most remarkable day in the life of an infant, from a psychogenetic point of view, is the one in which he first experiences the connection of a movement executed by himself with a sense impression following upon it." This experience came to his child during the fifth month, when upon tearing a paper into smaller and smaller pieces, the child noticed on the one hand the lessening size of the fragments, and on the other, the noise which accompanied his act. In the 13th month, he found pleasure in shaking a bunch of keys. And in the 14th, he deliberately took off and put on the cover of a can 79 times, without stopping for a moment's rest. Still later, he enjoyed pulling out, emptying, refilling, and pushing in a table drawer, heaping up and strewing about sand and garden mold, throwing stones into water, and pouring water into and out of bottles, cups and watering pots. It is easy to see that each of these occupations was for the young experimenter both a step in the discovery of his own selfhood as a causative agent, and a step in the interpretation of external objects.

I think this statement is satisfactorily down to earth, and might balance many of the statements that one can't help feeling uncomfortable with because of the high-flown style in which the human soul was discussed. Not that the human soul shouldn't be discussed in a high-flown style, but every age has its own fashions in these matters and ours have changed pretty radically since the Victorian ethos of the late 19th century.

Actually, the part that is hard to take in Miss Susie's writings is the burden of reliance on what is conceived to be the symbolic character of all the Froebelian apparatus and the Froebelian thinking. The games, the Gifts, the Occupations are things that are supposed to guide and clarify the child's budding soul, to put it in tune with the destiny of spirit, which is somehow already out there in the big world, hovering over the waters. Yet when I think of much of what has happened in education since that time, I look hard to find a better framework for inviting perceptive teachers to see their children as already embarked on a unique and individual history or to conceive their day-to-day learning as incidental to a unique profile of talents to be fostered, disciplined, combined, brought to interaction with the talents of others. Let me quote one more place from Susan Blow's essay on the meaning of play. This is a very brief statement, a summary of her principles, and I ask you to think about its adequacy from your own point of view. "The kindergartner," by which she always means, incidentally, the teacher not the child—we refer to children as kindergartners, she refers to the teachers as kindergartners; they're gardeners, you know, they run a garden—"the kindergartner who has insight into Froebel's idea of man as *Gliedganzes* (the participant whole) must expect and welcome a complicated task. Two thoughts she must keep ever before her. The first, that every exercise she gives should incite and develop self-activity. The second, that in every exercise she should strive to multiply the power and knowledge of each member of her class by the power and knowledge of all its other members." That's her summary.

As a sort of final commentary before I leave Miss Susie, I would like to share one other quotation from her work, which I personally find very enjoyable. The title of this section is "The Worst is a Corruption of the Best":

> It is a sad thing for anyone who has mastered Froebel's principles to witness the perverted application so often made of his Gifts. In many kindergartens, the sole thought seems to be to use these Gifts for teaching the elements of form and number; in others, manual dexterity is the one object sought, while in still others, the material of the Gifts suggests tedious object lessons on wood, iron, paper, wool, and straw. One kindergartner catches the idea of sequence and, forthwith, she arranges a series of forms and drills for pupils to repeat them. Another conceives the plan of using the Gifts to illustrate the songs and proceeds herself to work out exercises showing what the wind did, or what the pigeons saw. Finally, the kindergartner, who is really a disciple of Rousseau, though she imagines herself a follower of Froebel, blandly leaves the children to their own devices, and whether they build up or tear down, whether they work with or without purpose and interest, stands aloof, serene-

ly confident of the magic power of wooden cubes, sticks, and tablets. Seeing these things, one ceases to wonder at Froebel's remark that if, in 300 years after his death, there should be in the world one kindergarten like that in his mind, his fondest hope would be more than realized.

Well, I didn't want to talk mainly about Miss Blow, but, in a sense, she does provide me with something I would like to bring up without any elaboration. It stems from this rather high-flown Hegelian background. I'm sure many of the people here today who have worked back into the literature as far as John Dewey are thinking at this point that possibly Dewey had some influence on Susan Blow. And, if I may continue this time reversal of historical influence, Dewey might even have had some influence on Froebel. If the philosophy were shorn of its idealist language and read instead in terms of some of the actual practice of these early kindergartens—the way in which they actually dealt with children and communicated with them and the kind of environment they created for them to inhabit in those gardens—one can find a good deal of Dewey in Blow and Froebel. Indeed, in Dewey's Chicago curriculum, one can find a good deal of Froebel, particularly Froebel's belief that children should gain their freedom by reenacting the history of the race; that is just what the curriculum was in that Chicago school.

In *The Child and the Curriculum,* Dewey conducts a fascinating discussion of that relationship, but he never once gives a concrete illustration of a particular child or a particular bit of the curriculum. And that's what I mean by his "abstractness" and his emphasis on method detached from substance. In the Chicago experiment, Dewey did indeed commit himself to substance, to a curricular framework. In fact, it was a rather more rigid one than most of us today might think proper. But at least it was a framework that was conformable to a view of child development, and to a view of the evolution of mankind, of man's place, and of human need in the 20th century. But that part, the curriculum, was not argued anywhere by Dewey, as far as I know. It was simply taken over from the progressive world view of Dewey's time, and I suspect taken over from Dewey's own Hegelian past.

Another way of being dissatisfied with Dewey's middle-stage preoccupation with process, with flow, with method, so much of which we've heard recapitulated in recent years, was offered once by Professor Woodbridge, who was Dewey's powerful colleague when he came to be professor of philosophy at Columbia. What is *problematic*—I paraphrase Woodbridge who used Dewey's favorite term—is set always in a context which is *not* then and there problematic, though that context itself may later give rise to other problems not yet defined. Woodbridge's conception of philosophy was not the analysis of method, not the phenomenology of thinking, which was Dewey's central focus. Woodbridge's central focus was on trying, for his own age at least, to define a context for the problematic, which would itself not be problematic, which would be stable; a context of what is known, what is assured, what is important and unified, so far as possible, in its conception of man and nature—what Plato taught us to call "the nature of the good." That part of the philosophic task, I think, is missing from this middle period of Dewey's, and it is only toward the end of his life that it begins to be built up. In his writings on education it isn't there except by implication. If you know something of Dewy's outlook on life, something of the streams of thought and influences he shared and participated in, you can impute a kind of cosmology, a view of the universe and man's place in it, to Dewey. But he doesn't discuss these things and he doesn't relish their discussion. He tends to relegate them to older and outmoded traditions of dogmatic philosophy, which he thinks science has replaced.

Oddly enough, it seems to me, this is a very good time in history to be talking again about these ideas, these experiences. We've gone round the circle. We've not only gotten over some of the old dogmatisms, but we've gotten over getting over them. And it may be time to start thinking clearly again about this question of the unproblematic background that we ought to try to define as a context for our discussions of the substance of education. It has two poles. One of them is our whole preoccupation and concern with child development, with the uniqueness of the human individual, with self-activity, which is the essential causality of human development in its interaction with a social environment. That's one part which all teachers will take seriously and pursue in their own thinking and in their own investigation. But there's another part of it which is on the agenda, and it seems to me this is the time we should come around to it.

It seems to me perfectly clear that we can replace the agenda of the 19th century's pious idealism by something much more exciting—something much more challenging, and certainly not something to be complacent about. We can say that, from here on out, there is going to be one central preoccupation for human beings, for which we must, at all costs, prepare ourselves if we are to develop a culture which is a happy culture in any way, if we are to lead lives which are in any sense good lives—that is the task before us of becoming something that we have never really thought much about: becoming the custodians of this planet. I find in that conception a challenge fully equal in scope to that of the 19th century Hegelian march of spirit, which we now can see was immensely parochial, immensely narrow, immensely limited to a tiny part of the European peninsula and its extensions into the New World, even while it took itself to be the whole world. The narrowness, the parochialism, we know, is on its way out, but it is still very much with us.

At any rate, when you start looking at the curriculum, which this custodial role of mankind requires from now on, it seems to me to be an adequately broad framework within which our efforts at self-education can be contained, at least for the time that we can foresee. I don't want to spell out all the details, but you can see what it involves in some rather traditional sorts of categories. First of all, it involves the sciences. Good lord, think about what we have not assimilated into our bones that come from the sciences. The context of our history, 10 billion years. Most of us find trouble thinking about more than 50; we get confused by big numbers like millions and billions. But that's part of it, the history of the planet; the astronomical context in which all of this happened is part of the new version of the story of the Garden of Eden, only it's worldwide, humane, and nonsectarian. In a sense, it is a marvelous myth, which happens to have the virtue, so far as we know, of being literally true. The origins of life, the evolution of life, the appearance of man, the evolution of culture—all of this is part of the background that we need to know and be acquainted with in order to face the world that we have to live in, and try to live in well. And that is a pretty radical reconstruction—to use one of Dewey's favorite terms. In addition to the biological and physical sciences, there are the social sciences. We must, as a culture, as a community, learn to assimilate these things easily, and enjoy them, not simply to learn about them as technical, crabbed subject matter, of no interest to anybody, except so-called specialists. Then, of course, there are the humanities—the attempt to recover from all of our past experience the kinds of virtue and the kinds of ability and the kinds of talent that we now see so desperately needed in facing our future.

If you take the implications of all of this and bring them back to the early learnings of young children, what is it that you're going to find underwritten by the consideration of this framework? I have to leave that with you as a question. In most of the talk about progressive education, about open education, partly because of the influence of the rebels, these things are perhaps taken for granted. But in not talking about these things, and not making them explicit, there's also the danger that they are not taken for granted, and that what we substitute is a kind of curriculum of subjectivity, of alienation, of preoccupation with ourselves and the fascination of our views of each other's psyches, without any relation to this big world in which we have to live and survive.

On the plains (here, northwestern Nebraska in the late 1800s) the one-room schoolhouse usually was built of sod and in Spring sported a roof of sunflowers. Library of Congress.

Salter School, Athens, Georgia, circa 1900. Schomburg Library.

Blanche Lamont with her school in Hecla, Montana, October 1893. Library of Congress.

The One-Room Schoolhouse—South

If someone couldn't read, you just spent a lot of time with him. I laugh remembering one of my brothers, who now would be considered, I guess, a slow learner, but who has since gone on to do some great things. We spent an awful lot of time each night going over the lesson with him. The teacher said that was what was to be done and it was set up in that way. In school, if you could read, you spent time helping those children who couldn't, while a teacher was working with somebody else.

MARY BURKS • Just for clarification, in case there's anybody here with a good idea of geography, the place is in Pennsylvania County, the nearest town is Danville, Virginia, just to give you some idea as to where it is. Most people start thinking about it in terms of southwestern Virginia, but back home we like to call it the beginning of the mountains. It's quite near places like Roanoke and Lynchburg. There we had a one-room school. It was closely related to what many of us today like to consider a community school. It was built as a result of some people getting together and thinking that the children in that community needed a school. The people who lived in that community provided the land and the building. The county provided them with teachers, but the parents retained the power to say to a teacher, "We no longer will have you in our schools." And when they said, "our schools," they meant it was their school.

If you looked at the pictures in Lincoln Hall as you came into this conference today, or if you looked at the ones from Georgia in the late 1800s, that's about what the school room looked like. There were rows of seats; they were all nailed down. A large stove stood in the center. And the teacher had the good sense to seat the smallest children near the stove. Everybody else fanned out from there.

I started school in first grade (there was no kindergarten in Virginia at that time) and was one of those disruptive students. I was thrown out by October, completely; unready and unfit for school. And when something like that happened, and on the basis of the kind of relationship that existed between school and home—the teacher generally either lived in the community or was very close to people in that community, there was a lot of parent participation in that school, and teachers communicated with parents—the teacher took me home to my parents one day and explained why I was no longer welcome at the school. My mother sat down and tried to explain to the teacher what she thought her child was all about and I was permitted to return to the school.

I was one of those students who went to school having been taught to read by older brothers and sisters. We also had a thing in that county where children bought their books; therefore the books were a part of the family from the time the first child went to school right on through high school. That meant that in August or so, parents started looking around for books for whatever grade level their child was going to be in. What happened often was that children went to school having read the complete reader or having done the complete math book. I guess it was a little difficult for teachers. But they say that necessity is the mother of invention. So the teacher then had to come up with some other things.

Children walked 10 miles to school. There was very little absenteeism. If somebody was out, it naturally meant that he was sick. I can remember having children escort me to school. We went from one one-room school to another. If it was thought that smaller children had too far to walk, somebody would walk with them. When my older sisters and brothers had gone off to high school, I can remember having kids walk me five miles one way—because I was too small to walk alone at that time—and then turning around and going back past the school to the other side to their homes. So people used

The One-Room Schoolhouse—South

their own resources to make sure that children got to school.

Generally, I think, we spent a great deal of time teaching each other. If someone couldn't read, you just spent a lot of time with him. I laugh remembering one of my brothers, who now would be considered, I guess, a slow learner, but who has since gone on to do some great things. We spent an awful lot of time each night going over the lesson with him. The teacher said that was what was to be done and it was set up in that way. In school, if you could read, you spent time helping those children who couldn't, while a teacher was working with somebody else.

We did not have a wide variety of facilities: nowhere near the manipulative materials that we have today. I think crayon, paper, pen and pencil were probably the basic things. It was a tobacco town and, therefore, later on, many children came to school after having worked what you would consider a whole day. By the time they arrived at school at 9 o'clock, they had already done a great deal of work. And when they left school, they went back home to do a great deal more work before 7 or 8 o'clock at night. I was lucky; I came from a large family, so I didn't have to worry about that. The joy of the whole thing was that most of us in that school read very well and some of us read exceptionally well. At different times, we even competed in county competitions.

There were probably somewhere between 30 to 60 children in a school, in that one room, depending on the time of year. That doesn't necessarily mean that everyone, at six years of age, started school. If there was a child along the way who was five or four and was a little anxious to go, he went also— if he didn't live too far from school to walk or if he had somebody to carry him. And, of course, there was only one teacher.

Most of those 30 to 60 children stayed all year; very few people did much moving. And that was one of the things that I always regretted: We never moved. We had one family in the whole school that moved and the joy of that family was that they always would cycle back to that school. We all always heard stories of what went on when they moved from the school.

As I said before, we were arranged in rows according to grades. And the stove provided the central point. Wherever the stove was, in whatever part of the building, that's where you could decide that the first grade would be, and then the others fanned out on each side from there. The mornings were taken up mainly with reading and math and in the afternoons we did projects. Academic work was divided up. We had social studies and geography on different days. You started studying them in the third grade, and by the seventh you had to know all about the world. Maybe on Tuesday and Wednesday we would have health, along with some other things. Sometimes we worked on joint projects. I can still remember doing a social studies lesson on Lincoln's Birthday, where somebody built the cabin and somebody else did something else. And it was sort of interwoven from there.

I can't remember too much about the science we did, except that there was a Science Fair during the year, which we participated in, and in preparation for it we did work on special experiments that the supervisor brought in for each person to try. I guess we lived most of our science right there with the planting and everything else, so we weren't too involved with that. The practical things of life you sort of learned at home. There was not too much brought in, in terms of cooking, sewing and that kind of thing. People learned that at home. Music consisted of general singing. There was a piano in the school and one of the teachers played it, but generally our musical education was just singing, folk singing, or that kind of thing. Dancing was not popular in that community, so we didn't do any.

We played games during recess. There were three recess periods, including one in the morning. I remember eating up my lunch during the 10 o'clock recess and having to share my sister's lunch at noon. There was no such thing as part of the people having recess and part doing something else. The teacher had to be with you at recess, and she couldn't manage outside if half the children were inside. But if you wanted to stay inside and read your book, that was up to you, provided you weren't the type of child who might get into mischief. Lunchtime was at 12 o'clock; that was the standard thing for the community. Everybody around there, on the farms and everywhere, ate at 12 o'clock.

I still remember, during that recess time, doing things like playing house, which meant selecting a number of trees and setting up a string around them to divide off a room. We had all the rooms that were in our own houses, of course. The teacher came in and sat with us when we acted out those kinds of things. We went through the same roles that we had seen our parents perform.

Today we talk a great deal about parent participation in the school program. There was certainly a lot of that. On Saturday nights, parents used to have anything from a ham sandwich selling to a hog call to a fish fry, whatever, to raise money to provide things for that school. I can still remember our first commercial swing. We had swings in the trees, but that was our first set of store-bought swings. It was a memorable event. And parents thought in terms of the community, not just their children. One of the things that I remember well is this one lady coming to school to get on this particular teacher, saying "I didn't come just for my children, I came for every child in this school." When one parent came to school, nobody else in the community needed to come, because she spoke for everybody in that community. And it wasn't always the same parent. I don't mean they said, "Well, look, Miss So-and-so is going to be the spokesman." But if you had to come to see about your child, then you spoke for everybody. And that was the general thought at that time.

Mainly the parents visited. They came to see what was going on and such. If there was a problem, they came. The big thing was that the parents provided the school with financial support. They often came in to help with plays, all kinds of productions. Graduation was a big thing, as you can well imagine. They often provided lunch for children during the daytime on special occasions, such as softball games. The parents came and brought lunch for that. Also, there were a number of one-room schools in that area and from time to time the parents would get together and just spread lunch and have children from other schools come in. That would be a way of keeping in touch with other schools. But I don't remember any parent teaching, as such, in the school system.

What happened from then on, after a certain period of time, I mainly think of in terms of politics. You see, if you gave your land to the school, and you built your own school, then, in fact, it was your school. But later on, people thought that that gave some people too much power, so they consolidated the schools. Now they have what, I guess, we think of as a small school still—they have 10- and 12-room schools—but certainly the community is larger. And instead of going from first through seventh grade, they have what they call middle schools—primary schools, and middle schools, and then high school.

Everybody learned to read by reading the one newspaper in town, or by having it read to you by your parents, if your parents could read. In some areas, if you were lucky, the minister's wife was also educated. Then you received a wide variety of reading materials. Some people joined churches on the basis of what they felt about their children. If they were interested in education, often they joined the Presbyterian Church and received materials from the New York Bible Society. And then, of course, there was the little pamphlet that went with every Sunday School class. Many children, I'm sure, learned to read by reading the Bible, hard as some of us think that is to read today. Also, you had to read catalogues to understand about ordering seeds, about lumber. I can still remember my grandfather being able to look at a tree and tell you how many feet of lumber it had. So you had to know about all those kinds of practical things for living. And those were the things that you read.

There was no public library. The only library was the library that the teacher and the minister brought into our community. On the other hand, it wasn't so strange for us to have our own books. It depended on your having the type of parents who bought books, as I can still remember my mother doing. Not only did she buy us books, she bought the neighbors books. She also worked in the school system and often got books from it to bring home to us. And we shared them. That was something else, people weren't very selfish. I mean, 'What is good for my kid is good for everybody else's' was the prevailing ethic.

In reading, we relied on two things. We had a speller that went into all the rules, which I learned pretty rapidly but still didn't know what they were all about until I started teaching myself, I guess. And mostly a sight word approach was used.

Whatever a child could figure out with another child to help him learn to read was pretty much what was done.

There was no such thing as a noneducable child. If a child went to school, he was supposed to learn to read. We had a supervisor who came around and asked the teacher who could not read. And if the child had come to school a certain number of days, he was supposed to be able to read. It was never questioned. I guess that was the good part about it. No one ever said, "Well, he may not learn to read." Reading was considered a skill and the more you practiced it, the better you were supposed to get at it. If you couldn't read, it just meant a few of your chores would be shortened so that you could spend more time on it at home and at school. People just spent more time talking to you and making sure you learned to read.

The classes were graded but it depended on the teacher and on the child at that moment. From first through second grade was quite cut and dried. Then, in third grade, we were divided up. Half of us moved ahead and the other half sort of stayed behind, at least in the beginning of the year. My brothers had what they called an 'A' or 'B' of the grade, so that part of it went along, and the other part stayed behind. Some children were skipped, if your parents believed in that. I came from one of those schools where parents didn't believe in skipping children, so it didn't happen too much there.

No one got promoted automatically. Some children did fail. But children seldom failed more than once. I can still remember one little boy who did fail first grade. And something happened to him, I guess, in the second grade. He shaped up or something, or people spent more time with him, or something, and after that he was promoted. The only thing I can remember about this child was that he hadn't finished all the readers. I can remember we had such a large number of readers for first grade. You started with the primer and we must have had five readers or more. I think there were three softbacks and two hardbacks: Dick and Jane this and Dick and Jane that, and so on.

It was a pretty stable community—mainly large, well-run families. You couldn't have eight children and have them all not be pretty well disciplined. I'd like to qualify that because

I think sometimes, when you say that, people think of really strait-laced parents. I can still remember my mother saying to one teacher, quite clearly, "I don't need you to discipline my children; you tell me about it and then I'll handle it from there." A teacher in the wrong didn't last very long. One teacher thought it necessary to discipline the children in that school and she wasn't with us the next term because of that. On the other hand, there was a standard at that time, and you, as a student, were expected to measure up to it. There was naturally good discipline because the teacher had direct contact with your parents. Not only did she have direct contact with your parents, so did other parents. I still remember having my mother tell me I could stay out 'til maybe 12 o'clock and then having another parent tell me I couldn't. I took the word of the parent who told me I couldn't because she told me that after my mother had given me permission. You see, what happened was, you were not only disciplined by your parents, you were disciplined by the community.

How did children feel about going from this one-room school to the larger high school? Well, I think people approached it with mixed emotions. Certainly it was a stepping out, but it also meant going 30 miles farther away. And that meant catching a bus. I can still remember a child saying, "I'll never make this trip again" after the first day of school. Many children got on the bus at 6 o'clock in the morning and did not return home until 6 o'clock in the evening. The school day ran from nine to three. We called the bus trip "the nonstop 30 miles one way."

We laugh about it now, but many of us really looked forward to it because, still, it was another step in life, another challenge. We started out with, I think, about 400 people and ended up with about 100 and some. The people who fought the temptation to not make the effort, and who felt that education was a way ahead for their children, saw this as branching out. But there were some people who just couldn't face it, they just couldn't take 30 miles. Now we laugh. We say we probably learned more with the bus breaking down, and getting on and off, than we did in school, because we spent a great deal of time getting on and off.

The One-Room Schoolhouse—North

Being a one-room schoolhouse teacher, you weren't aware that you were drawing on your knowledge of a family for the day. It was just given that you understood, when Johnny came to school, where he was coming from and what kind of family he was coming from.

NEVA LAROCQUE HOWRIGAN ● I was born in Vermont, in a small town, and I went to a normal school for two years, after my formal education in grade school and high school. And while there, I was contacted and asked to teach in this small farming community near the Canadian border. It was a one-room schoolhouse, with eight grades generally, although the first year I had only up to seventh graders. After that I had the first graders that came into the school, right through the end of their first schooling.

Teaching in a small community in those days, you lived with one of your families. In fact, most of the children in my school came from the family I lived with. I had six the first year, and then seven the next year, because there was a new child beginning school. So you lived with them, and you had them in school. That's the big difference between there and what you get here in the city; you're very close to the children. We didn't have busing in those days. We started out from the farmhouse and went through a meadow and through the woods, and then across the field into our own school. In the fall, it was very pleasant. But as winter progressed, and there was more snow—some mornings we'd wake up and there was a big snowfall—then a team of horses would take us to school and make us a path on which to come home. So it was fun. But when you arrived at school it was very cold, and you had to start your own fire; you had to do your own housekeeping in this very tiny school.

The whole school was about the size of an average classroom, and it had a woodshed outside, and when you wanted to go to the toilet you had to go outside. There was no running water; you had to go and get your water.

When you went to school in the morning, you were preparing not only to teach for the day, but to be the janitor of the school as well, which meant piling up the wood. (In fact, a lot of the children ended the day piling up wood—what we called our "cleanup time." They'd bring the wood into the school for the next day.) You started the fire and you had to clean up because you were the janitor, and you got the janitor's salary, which, at that time, was about $9.25 a year. That was real salary, not inflated. My salary as a female teacher, was $570 a year.

How was I hired to be a teacher? I received a letter from the school superintendent. He had gone into my background and reviewed what I had done at school. And I was hired from that. I didn't have to go through an interview. He also obtained a boarding place for me when I went there; everything was set up. I never met him until after I got to the school. The superintendent had responsibility for many schools, in more than one community. But he would come and visit you, and encourage you, and observe what you were doing, to see if there were things that you might need in the school. There were about 11 or 12 students in the school.

I lived with two different families during the time I was teaching. I lived with one family two years. In those days— some 40 years ago—if the parents needed the children, they stayed at home and helped. We didn't close the school for everyone on that day. But I think a lot of the days off and vacations were community-oriented. For example, the school was closed for two weeks during the spring sugaring time, when a lot of the children were needed to help on the farms. We were also allowed to take off on snow days, although I never did.

You walked, and you just went through the snow. Perhaps if it was very, very cold you might not try to go in. You might call that a day off. I guess I just didn't mind it; when I was a child, I can't remember taking time off. But my children always looked forward to a stormy day, because this was the day you'd have off.

Small Vermont communities in those days found it hard to finance education. There were probably nine or 10 rural schools in a town and each had to have its teacher. Schools were scattered all over the area. So paying out salaries was quite a bit at that time. Moreover, the towns themselves employed the teachers, not the state; the superintendent was paid jointly by the towns he served. There wasn't even state aid, not really. In 1918, a man who taught made $20.75 a week in rural areas, and women, $14.35. And in urban areas, the salary was just about double.

My daily routine? Well, in my first year of teaching, I'm sure I tried to do things that I had been taught at normal school. But I think as you work along in that first year, and in your second and third years, you have to devise new things, considering the children that you have in the school, because certainly you can't teach everything to eight grades. So you work out and share your time with each of them. If you have some in first grade, you have to work with those, whereas your older ones can work by themselves. And then you supervise as much as you can. But you have to divide your time.

The curriculum of the school was determined by the fact that you had to do the reading and arithmetic and spelling, and you tried to cover these. You didn't cover them every day. There weren't the special types of materials—materials specially prepared for reading, say—that are available today. The town didn't have that much money for books and materials. You had to use what you found in your community and your school; and you had to make your own. There was a reading series, a program, but I've forgotten its name, it was too long ago.

We didn't have physical education. You didn't need it in those days. The children had just walked one mile to go to school, and they would have to walk back. And then in the winter, they had to tramp through three feet of snow. They certainly were getting their exercise. Not to mention their chores on the farm.

But the children loved to sing, so we would learn songs. It was a special occasion. I don't know if you would call it a reward. If everyone completed his or her work, then we would have a singing session, always on Fridays. I don't know why, but this would be the day. And we would try to do some art work, perhaps along with the season. It wasn't anything very much, I'm sure, compared to what you have now. We had colored paper and scissors and paste, and we tried to do things. Perhaps there might be something the children wanted to make and take home to their parents and show themselves.

We started school at nine, and since we were a mile from the school, we probably left home about eight because we'd want to start a fire going. In my third year of teaching, I walked two miles to school, which was really hard. The time walking to school, walking through the woods, wasn't wasted. We talked and learned about the things around us, and then shared with the other children when we got to school. You could see a farmhouse; the woods are right there, everything is there, you didn't have to go far to find things. You didn't have to bring so much into the classroom. You could go to it.

Did the older children help me? Sometimes. But you see, these children, I felt, had to spend most of their time accomplishing their work, because when they went home they had tasks to do; they couldn't take their work home. So they had to complete their day there. Of course, some children would quickly finish their work and then be ready for something else. They might be able to help a few others.

There's one thing I would like to say about the way people want to get outside and do 'nature studies' and things like that. Living on a farm, you didn't want to study Nature. You didn't need to go to school to do that. You didn't need a teacher to tell you these things. Your family was there and that's what you were doing each day of your life. These children, you know, had to cut wood, so they knew the different trees, they knew which ones could be cut and which should be saved.

My training as a teacher really was quite basic. No child development courses. One went to high school—and then you were asked to go to a normal school, if you could. Normal school was the equivalent of a higher education, which prepared you for teaching. Today it would be called a teachers' college. I don't know that you could say it was a well-rounded sort of education. We weren't exposed to any of Dewey's work, for example.

As a teacher, you were really on your own. You had to find your own way. The state set up a requirement, which you were supposed to try to convey to your children, but you were really on your own. You would try to remember everything they taught you, but all you could hope to do was work it in. One moment you'd have two or three children in a grade, then you'd have this one child in a grade, and you had to keep that one child interested. You know, they had no one to compete with, they had to do it on their own, so you had to make it interesting for the one or two children in a grade, and then just the one.

Discipline? It was never a problem. For one thing, we didn't have a large school. And, you know, these children just looked up to their teacher, they just respected her so much. You were their world and whatever you said they just believed. It was just very simple compared to the situation today—they did so much for their teacher. Of course, if any children were distracting the class, fooling around, not doing what they were supposed to, they were given something else to do; the boys might have to go out and pile wood for a while; the girls put their heads down on the desks.

There was no library. You'd bring a book and you would read to them; it would be something that would interest all of them. And they'd read to each other, repeating the books they liked best, over and over again, as they grew older. Most of them learned to read. They weren't restricted in their reading to a particualr grade level. If a child was advanced, he joined a more advanced group of readers. But, you know, most of them really needed to take each grade as it came.

We got to know the children very well, having them for many years on end. I mean, you knew what to expect from each one, and you knew what abilities each had. Sometimes children had to repeat work, but it didn't carry the onus getting left back does today. In fact, the children were used to repeating work, being in the same classroom for so many years. When you're all together, you can't help being interested in the other children's work. And that part was helpful because when it came to be their work, they had a better grasp of it.

Being a one-room schoolhouse teacher, you weren't aware that you were drawing on your knowledge of a family for the day. It was just given that you understood, when Johnny came to school, where he was coming from and what kind of family he was coming from.

Class in one of the "moonlight" schools for illiterates in Kentucky, circa 1915. Teachers volunteered their time and prepared weekly newspapers of local and school events for use as reading texts. Library of Congress.

Moonlight School Classroom. Founder of the schools, Cora Wilson Stewart, argued that public school "has no right to say to men and women, 'If you embrace me not before a certain age or before a certain hour in the day I will close my doors to you forever.'" Moonlight Schools for the Emancipation of Illiterates, by Cora Wilson Stewart, E. P. Dutton & Co., New York, 1922.

Highlander

... the boundaries people accept are always unnecessarily restrictive. We think everybody can push the boundaries out far, far further than they ever dreamed of. People who live too limited a life don't dare do things, they don't dare think or stand up for their rights, they don't dare explore or be creative or not conform.

MYLES HORTON ● The idea of the Highlander Folk School, which grew out of the early years of the Great Depression, was to try to use adult education as one of the main mechanisms for changing society. I had come to see that it was wrong for adults to always say: "The younger generation is going to change society," and then for them to go ahead and fix it so that it would be impossible for the young to do just that. I decided if you're going to do anything about changing society—through education—it has to be with adults. And I still believe that that's the only way educators can make a contribution, if at all, to change society.

We decided to move into a mountain area and establish a regional base to deal with adult problems, whatever those problems were perceived as by the people in the area. That doesn't mean we didn't have certain values of our own, certain ideas of our own. We did and do. We wanted to have a place where people could come freely regardless of sex or race. In fact, we had a combination of all ages because of the connection we had with community programs and extension programs. One way or another, we reached everyone, starting with Claudia Lewis's kindergarten kids, and even before that, and all the way through the span 'til we buried our neighbors. In fact, all the tools for the funeral were kept at the school. So we took care of the birth and the burial. I guess that's a good way to describe it. The school hasn't changed a great deal since that time. It did move from one county to another, but we're still in the East Tennessee mountains. And we're still trying to do something to help the workers in that region.

As in the past, our efforts overflowed. They overflowed from that county to neighboring counties, to working essentially with the industrial union movement of the South—the CIO and the emergent labor unions. Later on, our work overflowed beyond the boundaries in connection with a kind of pre-Civil Rights program, one of the programs being discussed at this conference, the Citizenship Education programs that Martin Luther King's Southern Christian Leadership Conference took over from us. Then during the Civil Rights period, we got pretty deeply involved, like many of the people who were active at the Highlander School.

That's the fairly recent phase of the Civil Rights movement. I think there's always been a movement, but I think the one that we're most familiar with was sparked by Mrs. Parks, who came to Highlander about three months before she refused to move to the rear of the bus in Montgomery, Alabama, and by a lot of the people who became leaders in SNCC or SCLC or one of the organizations in the South connected with Highlander. Highlander was the only integrated place in the entire South, you know; we had kind of a monopoly. We knew practically everybody who was doing anything. They asked us why we were integrated. We told them we were too poor to be segregated. We couldn't afford two toilets, two rooms, two tables. We were poor. So we just had to mix everybody up. By that time, a lot of people knew about Highlander and when things started moving they came to where they were free enough to have solidarity with people, instead of trying to figure out the people.

So we became involved with the Civil Rights period, after which we tried to get back to where we started, to our own region, tried to do something there with the people. We think of our people as being a kind of subculture. Appalachia is the biggest gathering of poor white people in the United States. We feel we have a lot of kinship with the other poor peoples around the country—blacks, the Indians, the Chicanos—as well as with people in other parts of the world. We maintain relations with other parts of the world. I think one of the important things to tell about is a Tanzanian workshop we had down there recently. We try to keep the people in our region informed of what's going on in other places, everywhere from New York to China, and we do it in workshops.

I can tell you briefly what a workshop is: It is a residential coming together of people, who live together for three or four days, or for two or three weeks. They include adults who are already active in their community, emerging as leaders; not top leaders, not official leaders, but emerging leaders. Many of them are functionally illiterate, but wise, experienced. They choose a topic or subject they want to deal with—it might have to do with welfare problems, strip mining, black lung, education, health, unions, co-ops—and then they select participants from their own people, the people they think will benefit from this, and these come to Highlander. In a real sense, they bring not only their subject with them, but they bring their curriculum. That curriculum is their experience. We do what, I guess, you would think of as peer learning. We think the best teachers of poor people are the poor people themselves. The best teachers about black problems are the black people. The best teachers about Appalachian problems are Appalachians, and so on.

We say we're going to have an educational experience, a learning experience, where people can learn from each other. There's some cross-fertilization occasionally, some mixing of the groups, but that's always by choice of the people who have asked for the workshop. Most of our workshops are on request. If the Indians want to have a workshop there and they don't want to have anyone but Indians there, we say okay. If they want to get somebody else, we say okay. We'll have to do whatever they want to do. The same with any other group.

These programs are worked out in a rather informal way. At present, our board of directors is made up of a majority of Appalachian poor. During the Civil Rights period, the majority were southern blacks. During the labor period, they were labor unionists. The board and staff kind of move along with whatever the major program is. And the board and staff and the people at Highlander help to kind of create the program. The program is an interchange between the people who come to Highlander, whether they work in the field or in the classroom. We don't make any distinctions. Staff members work both places. We think the educational program is a continuing start for poor people who come to get a little shot in the arm, and then go right back to their communities and continue their learning.

At Highlander, people sit down and learn from each other. We are not into individual action. We discourage people trying to improve themselves as individuals at the expense of other people. We value interdependent, rather than independent, learning. And we believe in groups working together, not only with their own neighbors but with all kinds of people, all over the world, who have something in common. The idea of interdependence, too, is based on what people can bring to the sessions themselves. We don't have legal information, or technical information, but we provide the person, the materials, movies, or something. We say we'll help you do what you want. If you ask for it, we'll provide it. But basically, you have to learn from one another, because that's where the real learning takes place. Learn so that when you get back to where you live, you'll continue to learn. That's the nature of the program.

In the early days, we had more of a community program than we have now. Claudia helped get that started with the nursery school she ran. The role she played was an extremely important part of the background of the whole program. There's no separation between these programs.

CLAUDIA LEWIS ● It was partly community work. The children I worked with lived there on this mountain plateau. We didn't run the nursery school at Highlander Folk School. We had it in a number of rather crude little houses. And those were days really of great poverty down there, at the time of the Depression. I went down in 1938 and stayed until 1941. You hear a lot about working with disadvantaged children these days. I've often said to myself, my experience down there was a very early experience in working with so-called "disadvantaged" children, or children of the poor, children of poverty. And I have carried away with me some things that I have learned from that experience, that I thought might be helpful to tell you, since we were thinking about this today.

One of the most important things that happened to me down there, something I remember so strongly, was how I could count on those poor parents. They loved this little school, their children loved it. And so they supported me. They had nothing, really. They were extremely poor in those days. Maybe they had $200 annual income. Some of those who lived near Myles's school even took turns cooking the soup that I got from surplus commodities. Just in every way they stood by me. If the parents liked the school, if they felt you were doing something very good for their children, you could count on their support. I had that experience in a few other places, too, by the way. I went down to Mississippi for a few days to help with Head Start training. The way those parents pitched in and kept the thing going was nothing short of impressive. Some Indian groups out on Vancouver Island, in British Columbia, felt they had to have kindergarten for their children, they did so poorly when they got to the public school. They felt their children had to have kindergarten experience first. Well, they had a hard time getting money, too, believe me. But when there wasn't money to pay the teacher, they got together and made sweaters and had a bazaar. That's how it was in Tennessee.

Now, I'm going to tell you some things that I've learned about the children of poverty. You hear about children of poverty: they like this, they like that, they don't like this, and so on. Well, my little children down in Tennessee had some deficits, too. They didn't have the best of health. They came to the little school with their noses running all year long. They were poor. Many of them developed their language very slowly, it seemed to me; they talked baby talk. They called me "Miss Sewis."

Anyway, I learned to look for their strengths, and they had a great many. They were good at practical things, they had practical know-how. The first winter down there, we had a great big potbellied coal stove. One day, my little five-year-old, Charles Williams, went walking to the stove door, took a look, saw it needed some coal, got the shovel, put the coal in.

Well, I was just aghast. I wasn't expecting a five-year-old to do that. He handled it better than I could. And I realized that these children were used to these practical things. This is what they did at home. Their physical coordination was excellent. Better than the children I had worked with in New York.

Also, they were quite capable of taking a lot of responsibility for the younger children, and did so, often. I remember the day that our car ran out of gas. I used to collect these children for the Highlander Folk School. It was much too far for most of them to walk. Something happened; I think somebody had siphoned off some gas and we didn't have a gas gauge. Anyway, the car stopped and there I was, you know, on one of those rural roads, and all those little children. So we just started walking from house to house, the whole troop, a great long walk. And one of the children, who was nearly six at that time, picked up the smallest child and carried him piggy-back, realizing that little Franklin was too small to walk that long distance. I didn't ask him to do it. He just automatically did it.

I remember the day, too, that little Beverly came out to the car with her five-year-old brother, and her mother said, "Oh, she wants to go to school so bad; we know she's not quite old enough (she wasn't even two yet), but Billy will look after her, and if she's any trouble, we won't send her again." But Billy did look after her, all that day. Really a five-year-old protector, very responsible for her. So this was something excellent that those children had. The way they could take care of babies amazed me. I can even remember seeing a baby at a school meeting. I think the baby's parents were putting on a play and they got their older son to take care of the baby. There he was—he must have been about 11—sitting in the audience and the baby on his lap. And I noticed when that baby began fussing and whining how skillfully this little boy handled him, doing all the things any mother would do, diverting his attention. He knew how to take care of that baby just beautifully. Well, those are some of the strengths those children had.

I'll tell you about one thing that I learned as a teacher when I went to Tennessee. When I went there from the Bank

Street School for Children, where I had been teaching, it was my expectation that children in nursery school begin the mornings with activities. You know, a good voice period, either indoors or out. And then they'd have a period of lunch, snacks, stories, or something like that. And then they'd have another period of activity until school let out at 3 or 4 o'clock. Well, I had to learn something different in the mountains. When the weather got cold, the children would come into school and pull the benches and the little rough chairs we had close together, saying in so many gestures, "We want to get warm: it's cold at home, cold at school." They would get some books to look at; some of them wanted me to read to them, some of them were content to sit there, looking at you, getting warm. I didn't say anything. I could see that I was dealing with a different group of children from the ones I was used to. The way these needed to start this kind of day, sometimes for as long as a half hour or 45 minutes, was sitting there getting warm, before they were ready to start the activities. So teacher learned. How well you learn varies the curriculum and the programs for them.

I learned something about block-building, too. I had come from children, about age five, who were such wonderful block builders, they loved it. All over the floor, you could see the most marvelous constructions: the Empire State building, bridges, roads, everything you would see in the city. Well, we had some blocks in Tennessee. A friend had sent them down. But the children didn't use them as much as I expected, nor did they ever become expert builders with blocks. I came to realize that because they didn't live in a community where they ever saw the Empire State building, or other great exciting kinds of buildings, they wouldn't be moved to reproduce these in blocks. Children are different in different places and you should have different expectations of them. Nor did these children have blocks to practice on for years, as do most of the Bank Street children.

What kinds of activities did our children enjoy? Children are very much alike anywhere, provided they're interested. The ones I worked with in Appalachia played indoors, they played house. We had some of those cars. They loved to run cars along a little block road and have the cars smash up and get into trouble. I think this little ride they took with me in my car in the morning was sort of frightening to some of them. Were they afraid that we'd get into a wreck or something? I don't know. We'd get stuck now and then—in the snow or on a muddy road—and this sort of worried them. Anyway, they would play house. We had dolls that I had gathered at Christmas, crude things, most of them. We spent a lot of time outdoors. We had swings. We had some other kinds of apparatus. We had very big packing cases and boxes. They pretty much liked the same things as children in our culture. We had paint, very crude in the beginning. I'd take red dirt out of the road and put it in water. Very crude paint. But they undoubtedly loved painting and were crazy for the paint, however inadequate. We dug clay right out of clay banks, right from the school. They loved clay.

As nearly as I can figure it out, some of these children stayed babies in their language quite a long time. Possibly it was because at home nobody thought there was anything wrong with their delayed speech, or baby talk, and so they kept a kind of baby talk, which they slowly grew out of. I didn't try to do anything about it directly. They heard my speech, and I read to them a great deal; they loved that. And sometimes they'd go home and tell their parents all the stories they had heard from me at school. They had what I would consider reasonably interesting and picturesque speech. Elizabethan words. They were people who speak very, very vividly. Oh, I can't think what right this minute, but their talk was just constantly full of interesting, wise language. And the children are raised with it. All I did was to talk myself, and talk with them; even Myles would read and talk to them. Gradually then they grew away from their baby talk. There were some extremes, obviously, children who would not say a word for months. A lot of the trouble was their shyness. They'd be shy with people who spoke a completely different way, with an accent such as they had never heard.

The thing that seemed to mean a lot to the parents was that their children have a chance to play together. I felt that that was one of the most important things that I did do—give them the chance to be with each other and play together. Otherwise they didn't have much contact with each other. It was no different from what I had tried to develop in any other school in any other state. They were learning to be curious about things, asking questions, taking little trips, exploring things, finding out what they could, enjoying stories, enjoying material. Mine were just any nursery school teacher's aims; they weren't any different down there.

How did you deal with the problem, or challenge, of talking to the larger community so that they would understand what you were up to, so that, at least, they'd allow you to go ahead with what you were trying to do, or, still better, support what you were trying to do? I know the survival of Highlander was often involved, having been burned down many times.

HORTON ● How did we cope with the problem of communications in the community? What we did was uneven. In the early days down there, we didn't have opposition from the local people. People were very poor and we identified with them. Actually, we went through a period of making a lot of academic mistakes, until we started learning about the people. Then we all got on a good basis and started relating. We helped them with their problems, we identified with them in their struggle. For about 15 or 20 years, we helped build a base of local strength. We built an independent political group that took over the county government. We organized unions and cooperatives—all kinds of programs. It frightened the coal companies and state authorities. They got busy about us and they got scared, and the burnings started. The white/black situation at the school was aggravating some people, not so much the local community as the people outside. So you make enemies, but you build friends; you build support.

Highlander always had the support of the community. Highlander was never done in by the community. It was pressure from outside forces. In fact, Highlander was confiscated at one time, the whole town was confiscated. Governors of five states got together and ganged up on Highlander. And they had to bribe every local person to testify against us. They didn't have a single person that they didn't bribe, not a one. They couldn't get any one to just volunteer. They had to threaten to put them in jail or something. So we started with a welfare community and drew on power from outside. That's how you start. Then you build a broad base. We felt we had to start building a base among black people and labor. They were the ones we worked with. You build friendships and you make enemies as you go along. There's always opposition from people who don't like what you're doing.

We had enemies, but there was nothing they could do about it. They burned us down, investigated us, they even put us out of business—they thought. And we just kept going. They don't bother us much now. You'll find that after 45 years, you wear them down. It doesn't bother me that we have enemies; it bothers me that they get so powerful and put us out of business temporarily. But I think if you're going to deal with social issues, you're going to be unpopular. And interestingly enough, the things that we were unpopular about are now accepted. They've become the law.

If you wait long enough to avoid getting people enraged or something—if everybody waits—nothing would happen. And, of course, you wouldn't have any problems. But that's not the kind of education we're interested in. We're interested in cutting into education. And I don't want to give you the impression that we don't deal with a lot of very practical sorts of problems. But we are dealing with people, unlike some schools that I know about. We say our job is to get people moving, and to get out of the way before they run over us—to start working with some other groups when we are no longer needed. We're kind of always on the borderline. And, of course, we've learned from the people we've worked with. That's a hard thing. You know, you get preconceived ideas, composed by people who get in the way of education, and that's their training, I guess. It's hard to get people to understand that we really want them to run their own program and do their own thinking, because all the education in this country—and I don't mean just schooling, but all kinds of education—sell people on the idea of fitting into a groove and being useful, turning out a product that can be labeled and certified and passed on. So we've had the problem of getting people to know that we really mean for them to run the program.

At Highlander, the students run everything—and have been

doing it for, well, not the first two years, we didn't know that then, but actually by about 1934 we were turning everything over to every group that came to Highlander, and they ran everything from the minute they got there until the time they left. We insisted they do it. They didn't like to do it, they didn't want to do it. And we didn't do a great deal of talking about things. For example, we were interested in cooperatives, to get people together, and instead of talking about it, we'd say, set one up and run it from the beginning, organize it and run it, keep the records, go broke, whatever happens. If anything would happen, they'd say, "This person's a troublemaker, what do you do? What do you do with it?" We'd say make that your problem. We turned everything over to them at the very beginning. That's the way Highlander has been running since 1934. We leave the decision-making to the people involved—and it still is as difficult as it was in the early days to get people willing to make decisions. Problem is they aren't allowed to make decisions, going into this playpen sort of thing we call schools to get certified.

We put our kids in the playpen or a crib and we haven't got the nerve to say to the little devils, if you get in our way, we'll lock you up: call it a playpen; it sounds better than saying crib. That's why I use that figure of speech. But it's really college graduates in a little more active playpen. You're never let loose until you get that top certification. But now you're an adult, now you're educated, now you can start making decisions. You never made one in your life about anything important, and now you make real decisions. How can people do that? So we have got to kind of undo, in our own way, our two cents worth, all this stuff that comes down on us from the outside.

Highlander, as I said at the beginning, is an adult school with the major emphasis on residential adult education. That's the main focus. We don't have any high school graduates and things like that. But when we're working in a community, we try to serve the community, the total community, and in the effort to serve that community, of which Highlander is a part, we had a nursery school and we had co-ops, we had gardens, and we had all kinds of things, including credit unions. We dealt with all the ages of that community. We had camps in the summer. We dealt with people outside the regular schooling system always. So, it's been an adult place primarily, but we've never drawn the line about who's supposed to be there.

We just tried to influence the educational systems in our region, developing and encouraging outlets and study groups. Last year, there were 40 common universities in our region that sent people to Highlander. We find that that is one of the ways of getting in—through the student—and counteracting all the mischief done by all the so-called good schools in the South you hear about, and read about, and send money to, which just package people for export—wrap them in cellophane and label them, and ship them off, get them ready to be useful to make some money, operate some program. We try to get the younger people and some of the more imaginative teachers whom you always find in any school—a small number, but they are always there—and kind of get in there and change things around. All the people on our staff come from the region, went to school in that region. We have got to be working on the inside. So we try to work on the colleges' problem and make a little headway there. Then we're on the other end with open schools, free schools, experimental schools. We try to encourage the development of all kinds of schools, in the hope of bringing to bear some of our influence on education. We've been part of some pretty good tussles down there. Some of our ideas are rubbing off in those places.

We believe that the boundaries people accept are always unnecessarily restrictive. We think everybody can push the boundaries out far, far further than they ever dreamed of. People who live too limited a life don't dare do things, they don't dare think or stand up for their rights, they don't dare explore, be creative, or not conform. We encourage people: if they want to sit on the front porch and whittle the rest of their life, I think that's a good thing; they might come up with some good ideas. And if you want to work hard, as long as you don't exploit anybody, that's fine with us. If you want to work parttime and live on a subsistence basis—that's your life style—we think it's fine. We try to encourage people to do what they themselves want to do and not let other people influence them so much, and that includes us. We say, don't pay any attention to anybody, including me. Start doing your own thinking.

I remember in pre-Civil Rights days, Hosea Williams, who was in SCLC for some time, was running this little program down in Atlanta, Georgia, and he invited me down to speak to the farmers. At first, I turned him down, and then he said if he couldn't get me, he would get somebody else. So I went down—I knew I was as good as anybody else he could get—and I got up before these black people, country people from seven or eight counties around Georgia, and I started out by saying, "I hope I'm the last white man you ever ask to give you advice." That was in 1950. "I hope that you never ask another white man to come down here to give you advice. That's what you asked me to do. The advice I'm going to give you is not to take any more advice from a white man. Get busy and start making your own decisions and start thinking for yourselves, and while I'm here, since I took the trouble to get down here, I'll discuss how you go about making decisions, but I'm not going to help you make decisions, and if I ever find out you asked another person to come to tell you what to do, I'm going to sabotage you."

I went all over the South telling people just that. I'd tell white mountain people, tell black people, tell anybody I talked to. I'd tell them, make up your own minds, make your own decisions, start learning to run your own lives and work out your own educational program. I wrote a little script, or an article, or something, in which I responded to the question: "What do you do about schools today?" I said, "Close all the schools down in the United States and take all the teachers that know anything about education, and get them out to educate the people about how to make decisions, any kind of decisions. Spend about two years learning to make decisions, here, there, and everywhere, and then come and tell your congressman the kinds of schools you would like to have. That's what I would like to see happening."

Poor people know that school certificates have to do with jobs. If you get a certificate that says you went through grammar school, you get a certain level job. If you've been through high school, you get a certain level job. If you've been through college, you get a certain level job. They also know that it has nothing to do with the quality of the education. They know that a Harvard Business School graduate who can barely get by gets the same job as the one who can, and they know it from their own experience. They know it has nothing to do with the quality of the education; it has to do with certification. So they want certification. And they want less "schooling" and fewer tests. The schools have the power to certify people as being educated. Poor people want their kids to get out of the poverty they've had—and they know that the certification is necessary. They want their children to go to school whether they learn anything or not. They want that certification, and if they could find somebody to give it to them without their going to school, they wouldn't be interested in going to school, they wouldn't be interested in education—the kind we have now. Then we could start over again and get some real education.

About 35 years ago, I proposed that everybody should be given a Ph.D. at birth and get rid of that problem right then. Then you'd spend your life getting educated. You wouldn't have to worry about grades or tests because you've already got that degree. It'd solve all the problems. Then you could get on with education.

LEWIS • Parent involvement? Let me tell you just a little more about the parental involvement that we had. At that time, we had some trouble with local officials. I had my nursery school in an empty room in a public-school building for awhile, and I was asked to move by the Board of Education, who obviously thought we were communists or something. Well, I was going to start packing up. I didn't think we could do anything about the board's decision. And some parents came by and said, "What are you doing packing up? We're not going to let you move. We pay taxes on this building. We want your school here. You're not to move, you stay here." Well, this is a long, long story. The board sent the sheriff down to padlock the school door and the parents heard about it and sat in front of the school for hours. We brought them sandwiches and coffee. They wouldn't let the sheriff come, even if he wanted to come. He *didn't* come (although the school board came and took my stove away). In any case, that's the kind of involvement that the parents had. They supported what they believed in and still do.

Now, your second question: did the parents' attitude towards children change? If it did, I wouldn't know how much. When I went around to their houses and talked to them, I never tried to talk with them about children's problems; they weren't aware of them. And I was treading very carefully. They were a proud people. Who was I to come in and try to do something that would make them think that I wanted to reform them? I didn't really. But I think they noticed certain things. For instance, they would say, "How come you have so much patience, you don't ever whip them." Well, I don't believe in the necessity for that, you see. They saw that I was handling the children in ways that were filled with love. I think maybe they learned something from that.

HORTON ● And they talk about that until this day. I've seen the effects of that nursery school. The things they learned from Claudia affected their lives, and some have passed it on to a second generation.

LEWIS ● There was nothing cognitively wrong with these children, nothing at all. Their environment was limited, but that's one thing I tried to clear up a little bit by taking them to a nearby city to see a newspaper being printed, by taking them to a garage to watch the whole process of cars—and talk about it—by broadening their horizons a little bit, because some of them never got outside of their own little yards. But they had natural curiosity.

How did they feel about being poor? I don't know how poor they felt. They felt very proud of themselves. Don't you think so, Myles?

HORTON ● These kids have been poor all their lives. The Depression hit the South and the mountains earlier than it did the rest of the country. They'd been in this Depression for at least 10 years before the nursery school got started. They had never gotten outside the mountains, and so they'd never known anything but poverty. They didn't know there was any other way; they had no alternative to choose from, no other exposure. Whatever exposure they had to alternatives was in the aims of the school; that was the only exposure they had outside of their homes. Their parents had never traveled much. Some of the children were in homes where none of the parents had ever gone outside the county. The kids didn't know much about anything *but* poverty.

Television may have brought in some images of the outside world, but I don't know how to analyze that. The people in Appalachia somehow have lost their pride—the poverty is there—but I don't think it's because of television. I think it's because, strangely enough, they're better off than they've ever been before. They have nicer houses. They have welfare. But the nature of the way the welfare is delivered, the nature of the way they are treated, demeans people and takes the heart out of them. Materially they're better off, but spiritually, they've been exploited by the very people—social workers, administrators, teachers, preachers—all the people who live off of them, or live on the basis of service; they have exploited and demeaned them, and it causes real degradation. When the black people finally could stand up against whitey and spit in his face if he got in the way, even the poor took pride in being part of a people. But we haven't had anything like that since. That's what I'm working on now, building pride on a basis of interdependence, not independence—that's outmoded. By working together, you help give the individual strength to stand up and believe in something bigger than himself, strength to try to get away from the business of loss of pride. A lot of that's been achieved since then.

The younger generation, the kids who have been to college, and who have been away at work, have decided to come back to Appalachia and live, to work hard, perhaps not to eat so well, but to live. A lot of the people have done that; the wheels have turned. For the first time in 35 years, there's an immigration in middle Kentucky, the coal mine area; that's not too well known. It's not too well populated either, but it will be as the people begin to try to make their lives there— the young people particularly. We had a workshop a couple of weeks ago; it started out to be a creative writing workshop. The people involved, though, wanted to turn it into a storytelling session—telling folk tales and making up stories.

They might be writing whole new stories now. I just got some stuff—two completely new stories about strip-mining and the war; old jack tales. They're getting back into something that's maybe very alive. This is the turn—something that looks pretty good. But the older people—they've had it beaten out of them. It's the price of having more material things; you get caught up with getting it until it degenerates the spirit. And they had to take it. I guess that was the nature of the pride. Now a lot of the people have to learn to dish it out.

What I think is wrong with the regular decision-making processes is that they're all so rarefied and stratified. You know, you say, "Here is an area where you can make a decision, here's one in which you can't." People are boxed in. After awhile their heart isn't in it. They say, "What the hell; it doesn't make any difference." And they're absolutely right. So they don't do it. If they do it, it's because they have a purpose in doing it. What seems to me crucial here—what it has to do with—is getting people used to making decisions: short-range decisions, long-range decisions, important decisions. Say we're going to decide something. I want to come into this room and make a decision during this session. Then I'm not going to get involved in making decisions about tomorrow and about running this place. If somebody else wants to get involved with long-range decisions, well and good; let people make any kind of decision they want to make, any time they want to make them, for as long as they want to make them. In other words, get people into making decisions, and set up processes in which this is possible.

A good example of how this works is what happened in the mountains in eastern Kentucky recently. A little community school burned down and the school authorities tried to consolidate it in a school 40 miles away; they put the kids in with 1,100 other people, and trucked them 40 miles to do it. And the people put up a fight—they always do. They opened up a storefront and got some old buildings, including the church, and ran it for three or four years—and they ran it themselves. It was fine, you know, they were using state money to pay teachers, but they were financing everything else. The state wouldn't build them a new building, said what they were doing was illegal (finally, you can't even educate people), you got to truck them over to this other place. Those people put up a fight for a couple of years and the experience educated the whole area around there as to how to run the school, how much it cost, how to deal with the board. They might have lost. Battles were lost on education before. But that community is a good community, a live community, a vital community, involved with something that means something to people, and they got the education, even with lost causes.

What Highlander has always said is that the power is in the people. Nothing new about that idea, nothing original about it, but the practice of it is kind of rare. We say *go to the people*. Like Claudia said, people came and wouldn't let them move her out. The people did that, they didn't have lawyers. They just had people who sat there, and that's progress. If you get people involved, then creativity comes out of people; it helps the "leaders" get things done. The power comes from the bottom instead of the top. Then people start educating each other, they don't have to expend their energy competing for power, trying to be manipulative. That's when you're going to get things moving. And that's what Highlander's done.

Ex-slave Jim Walker, over 100 years old, learning to read and write from a teacher in the WPA (Works Progress Administration), Birmingham, Alabama, circa 1939. Schomburg Library.

Star pupil, 82 years old, reading to her class in a WPA education program in Gees Bend, Alabama, May 1939. Schomburg Library.

The WPA Experience

... the only difference between a child's work and an artist's work is that the artist ... makes a breakthrough for the human race, but the little kid is making a breakthrough for himself ... he's making a discovery, he's opening up something new, he's reaching out, just for himself, but it's just as real a breakthrough.

EDWARD GLANNON • I had to quit school at about 14, and went to work in the mill in Pittsburgh. I worked in the mill, in stores, in factories, in an advertising agency. Then when the crash came, wham, no jobs. I had been awarded several scholarships in New York City, but being the oldest of a big family that needed the money, I couldn't use them. But when I was 21 years old, I got the Schakenberg Scholarship at the Arts Students League, which gave me the right to choose my teacher and about $14 a week, which was, at that time, an awful lot of money for a kid, and I came to New York, to work with Tom Benton.

In that same class were a lot of fellows who later had a large influence on the art world, among them Jackson Pollock, Willem deKooning, and the likes. We were all scholarship kids around there at that time. Or almost all. And when the scholarships ended—when the money that was supporting us ran out—Miss Croft, the director of the program, called us all in and said, "We can't pay you any more" (you see, we served as models, we served in the cloakroom, and we did the telephone operator's job), "we're broke. But I've heard that the College Art Association is going to hire some young artists." Well, it turned out that the U.S. Treasury Department had called on the College Art Association, the only association that existed at that time with any kind of status, and told them that they were willing to invest some money in art in New York, and that the association could pick the people. They just wanted it to be a relief project.

Well, Mrs. Clark, who was the head of the College Art Association, immediately took the kids who had scholarships and said, "You kids have already been screened; we'll put you to work. We'll pay you $19 a week, but you'll have to work hard, and you can have your choice: you can go on a mural project, which means you'll paint at home and deliver paintings to hospitals, or you can go on a poster project, which means doing posters for federal agencies and things like that, or you can go on a teaching project." Boy, that sounded pretty good. I thought I would like to be a teacher; I told her I wanted to become a teacher "this afternoon," and she said, "Those of you who are going on the other projects can go home and start, but anybody going on a teaching project will have to attend a series of lectures. They'll be given the next four days at NYU and I have arranged it with the man who will speak to you."

Well, we got down to NYU and there was a man there whose name I honor greatly, Hughes Mearns, and this guy was a nut on kids' poetry. He would ride around copying kids' stuff off fences; he bribed a lot of school teachers to save kids' poems for him. And I got from that man, right away, the gist of an idea, and I thought if this was the way school would be, I wouldn't mind going to school. I never saw anything like his enthusiasm. He would open a piece of paper and say, "My god, listen to this: 'Jack Frost sneered right down the street and he spat ice over all the houses.' Listen to that, listen to the zip in that." And he gradually gave us the idea that children could paint.

There was no art for children at the time. Mostly on Friday afternoon, the last 20 minutes, they drew patterns or something. But there was no concept that children were capable of making art. And Mearns gave us the idea in four days that the only difference between a child's work and an artist's work is that the artist—whether it's Cezanne or somebody like that—makes a breakthrough for the human race, but the little kid is making a breakthrough for himself. And he's making a discovery, he's opening up something new, he's reaching out, just for himself, but it's just as real a breakthrough. This is the thing you've got to watch for.

Well, after four days with Mearns, they sent me to the Gramercy Boys Club, which was in the old gashouse district—it's all gone now; it was where the Metropolitan Life housing project, Stuyvesant Town, is—and the director there was a Tammany politician who had no idea about art, except that artists were all communists; he knew that. He knew nothing about art, at all, but he was very much concerned about his kids and he wanted his kids treated properly. So he told me there were two things I had to do: "You've got to keep these kids from getting drowned in the East River, and you've got to keep them from hopping street cars. Other than that, I don't care what you do."

The only thing I knew and cared about was art, so they gave me a crew of little kids. I guess the oldest was maybe nine, or maybe eight; the others ran down to about five and a half, there was one who was only two. He came to the shop one night and an older kid had him by the hand. And I said, "Look, I told you, told you, told you, I don't want any little kids coming in here at night because the older kids will go away." He said, "Look, Mr. G., he gotta come in, I gotta watch him, he's my uncle!" So we had the uncle there, too.

These kids started to draw and paint, and in no time we were doing things. I was thinking of it a lot today. It was different in a certain basic way. The kids had lots of heroes, and what I did, trying to make friends with the youngsters in starting, I just went in and started to paint a mural on the wall, and I was painting different people, different sports figures, and kids would come around and help. They'd ask, "Can I?" And I'd say, "Okay, you can help." One by one, the kids joined up and we had a crew painting murals.

Now you can imagine what the attitude was about children's art at that time. We'd get nice murals, you know, beaver board. We'd go around Gimbel's at night, 1 or 2 o'clock in the morning, when they'd change the windows—Gimbel's, Macy's, Saks—and they'd bring out all this beaverboard, red velvet, all kinds of treasures, and we'd carry them back and paint on them, and things like that. Well, I can remember coming in and seeing my murals all sawed up to make partitions between the toilets. The director and assistant director of the Boys' Club didn't see any harm in that at all; it didn't bother them if that happened. If they needed a piece of beaverboard, they just cut up the murals. And it was very hard to educate them to the fact that a mural meant something and was symbolic of the importance of those kids.

We had a hard time getting started, but gradually these boys caught on and began to take art rather seriously. I took them to lots of museums and I took them to Coney Island once a week swimming. You see, I had a nice situation because I didn't have to take the place of a parent. I didn't have to say to the kids, "No, you can't do this, you can't do that." If they wanted to do something, I'd try to do it. It didn't matter what we did. It was the Depression and as long as you didn't hurt anybody, nobody bothered you. So I would be with these kids not like a schoolteacher—I met them at 2:30 p.m. and I'd stay with them until 10:30 p.m. And they were terribly poor. There'd be five boys in a family and only two would get to go out for want of clothes. Sometimes there would be one pair of shoes for the five boys, too, and the one that was being confirmed, or something like that, got to wear the shoes; the others would go without. But we could do almost anything we pleased. And one of the things we did very early—it's hard to believe this now, it's almost like another world—is to make tombstones.

There were a number of young Italian mothers who were very much ill-at-ease—even couldn't sleep—because their own mothers were buried in an unmarked grave. This was very serious business to these people; it was considered terrible, especially among the Italian women, to have a parent in an unmarked grave. But a marker for a grave was about $45; you just couldn't buy one. So we got the idea that we would make gravestones. And we went to the East River, where they were filling in all that land; they'd tear down mansions and just dump the stones there. Well, marble was the easiest thing in the world to get. So we hauled the marble off and taught the kids to carve. We made tombstones for anybody who needed them. And the kids got to be very good stone carvers. A lot of these kids are now sculptors.

Some of the things you had to teach them were so different.

For instance, I had to teach them how to flunk tests. Flunk them! This was during Mayor Jimmy Walker's time when the city officials were trying to economize as much as possible in the schools. If they found out that a kid could sew a button, they immediately took him out of his school and sent him to trade school, you know, to tailoring school. They'd give a kid a sign to paint and if he did a good job, they'd take him out of school and put him in sign-painting school. There were all these different trade schools around the city and they tried to dump the kids in there as fast as they could. Every once in a while some little kid would come in the shop with a long face and I'd say, "No, you didn't, you dope," and he'd say, "I didn't know it was a test." Then you had to go to Tammany Hall and get the kid back into academic school. You see, you had to go through Tammany Hall to get anything done. There was no other way. To get a kid in a hospital, you had to go through Tammany Hall, too. A lot of times, for instance, children would wear shoes that were too small. You'd meet a kid on the street and he hadn't been around for three or four days and you'd see his ankles hanging down over the tops of his shoes; he'd gotten an infection in his feet. After LaGuardia became Mayor, you could grab that kid and go right into Bellevue. There were no questions asked. But before LaGuardia became Mayor, you had to go to the ward leader. You always got in, but there was no other way to go, there was no other way to get a kid into a hospital even though it was a serious emergency like scalding; the mothers used to wash with a big boiler on top of the stove and every once in a while a child would climb up and pull that boiler over on himself. You still had to go through the political club to get that child into the hospital. It's hard to believe, but I lived through that.

The kids grew up with a nice sense of enjoying work. You see, we didn't have to be academic. We could do almost anything we wanted. We could go to the Bronx Zoo if we'd get enough nickels. If not, we walked. It didn't matter, night made no difference at all; we went day or night. These kids had no schedule. And I had no delinquency problems. I'll give you an example of that. There was an Italian sculptor down there and he got sick of listening to these kids yak, yak,

yak, you know; they talked, talked, talked, they never could stop; everybody in my shop talked all the time, everybody talked at once and it would never stop. This fellow was down there to help out for a couple of weeks, to sharpen chisels and teach us how to dress tools—he was a very skilled stone carver. The first day there, the kids talked so much the guy couldn't stand it, and he took a dollar bill out of his pocket and nailed it to the workbench and said, "Any kid that can keep quiet for five minutes can have it." You know that dollar bill stayed there for two years. Every once in a while a kid would come in and say, "I'm gonna keep quiet for five minutes, time me." You'd start to time him—about two minutes—he couldn't hold back any more; he had to say something.

But there was no kind of delinquency problem, we had nothing like that. One of the tragedies was that later all of these people were moved out, scattered to the Bronx, Staten Island, to every place, where they were not welcome. But there, they were home. A boy would say, "My mother was born in my house." It was home base. Also you had codes, you see. There were a lot of horses in the streets at that time and one of the dangerous things for a child to do would be to throw a stone at a horse. When any kid threw a stone at a horse, any woman on that block would pick that kid up, spank him, and say, "Don't you ever do that again"; and if she told the mother, the kid would get spanked again. Today, if you spank somebody else's kid, you'd be arrested. But then the mother would thank you for correcting her child according to the code of the neighborhood. This is the way we lived. You helped to instill that code in each other's children. And I think the reason that many of these people became delinquent later was that their roots were torn away. Delinquency grew greatly in the city because these people were all lifted away from their own roots, their own home plate.

Now, after about three or four years, my kids got to be pretty good painters. The first exhibition of children's art that was ever put on in New York, as far as I know—at the Museum of Modern Art when the museum was in the old Rockefeller home, right where it is now but in a different building—was formed by the pictures my kids painted. And the museum, in order to give the kids some kind of recognition, gave each kid a year's membership in the Museum of Modern Art, which allowed them to go there free, and to get copies of catalogues. Of course, a year went by very fast, and one day, all at once, the whole East Side nearly fell apart, because everyone of my kids got a bill for $150 to renew his membership, and the mothers were knocking at the door, "Look what you got us into! Now we have to pay $150!"

But the Museum of Modern Art show did an awful lot to help us get some status for children's work. It was no longer laughed at if the head was too big on a figure or if the kids did all kinds of oddball things. I can remember a kid once did a picture of a desert, and there's a little camel there and a guy's walking with the camel and he's got two great big suns in the sky. I didn't say anything; I was just looking at it. And he said, "You're worrying about the two suns?" And I said, "No, I'm not worrying." He said, "How many suns we got here?" I said, "One." And he said, "Hot as hell, right? Well, the desert's twice as hot." It was that kind of logic that you got used to working among these kids.

The man who was educational director at the Modern at the time was also educational director at the Fieldston School, he was rather torn and very busy because of it. The museum was pushing him to put in more time there and Fieldston was pushing him to put in more time there. So we worked out an arrangement where I would take his classes at Fieldston and he could put more time in at the museum. That's how I got permanently into teaching. In the meantime, at the Boys Club, the project ended. I went on the staff of the Boys Club as a gang leader, but I kept the same gang. I stayed with that same group of kids for nine years, until they went into the war. And they all came back, entitled to an education under the GI Bill. A lot of them went to college, for a year, two years, and some of them graduated and some of them have Ph.D.'s now. In the world that they lived in, they never would have expected to be able to go on to school. There had to be some guys who would say to them, "Now, look, you've got as much right to a college education as any other person in the world; all you got to do is prove to yourself that you can do it."

But we had a lot of adventures. One night President

Hoover walked into the shop. He was a kindly man and very understanding. He asked the kids, "Doesn't it bother your teacher that this is a little off perspective?" and the kids said, "No, that don't bother him. All he cares about, he said, isn't what the kid does to the wood—it's what the wood does to the kid!" "Well," Hoover said, "That's a very good explanation of what it's all about."

Sometimes people misunderstood. This sounds crazy, but when they tore down the old houses, those big slate sinks the houses had all landed in the dump, and we went there and got them, and we carved in them; we sculptured by the mile. Well, there was one kid who had a dead sense of reckoning. And he carved Abe Lincoln one afternoon, carved him tall and sitting on a horse, and his feet almost touching the ground. So we had open house one night and I put this kid's piece of work on exhibition; it was standing on a wooden block and looked real nice. And his older brother came along, who had never had any art education, and he looked at it, and he said to his little brother, "Did you do this?" And the kid says, "Yeah, I did it." And his brother hit him on the head, like that, and said, "You be more respectable of Lincoln! Put him in a coffin!"

But gradually the boys clubs and the settlement houses got to really appreciate the things that these children were doing, and realized that they were doing something for the lives of these children. And the neighbors, the people in the neighborhood, welcomed the artists. Among the kids, the artists had a kind of easygoing way. Many times, the teachers—particularly gym teachers and people like that in the settlement houses—were pretty rough on the kids. But anybody who treated those children with respect got unlimited love. These kids are now pushing 50 and I still hear from them. In fact, I saw something in a magazine the other day where one of them said that I had changed his whole life just by coaching him in art; he's now a professor in Philadelphia.

We had a good kind of anarchy in which the kids had a good chance to grow. We had no rules, we could make up our rules, and the kids were very appreciative. I can remember, for instance, the subway train at about 208th Street, where it comes out of the tunnel. Those kids would be sitting on the train and when it came out into the open air, they'd go, "mmm—trees." The odor of trees; they were so sensitive to that. I remember, too, that they used to make sandwiches with the long Italian bread and a fish in it. Any place we'd go on a trip, I'd have 40 kids on a subway car and all the kids had a loaf of this bread, like a clarinet, and they'd keep nibbling on it. By the time we'd get to Coney Island, it would all be gone, and the kids would be hungry.

I'm in a public high school now, but I still work as if I were on the WPA team. I guess I've learned to be an unorthodox kind of a teacher. I do enjoy the kids and it's very difficult for me to go by all the rules. So many of the rules require you to blame somebody for everything, and I don't know whom to blame, so I try to ignore it. But I found that the education that I got on the WPA stood me in very good stead as far as relations with children are concerned. It was a combination of all kinds of ideas, but I think Mearns helped an awful lot. Of course, I had read Thoreau, I had read Emerson, and things like that, but never with any concept of education in mind; I never thought of teaching kids. I think all the other art students who were at the Art Students League when I was there were much more confident in their art than I was. I had painted too many bad pictures. I was afraid that if I joined the project as a painter that I would do something really bad and be disgraced. But the teaching somehow seemed to fascinate me. It just seemed to work. It seemed to be the easiest thing in the world for me to relate to these little guys, and to stay with them for a lifetime. They're still my very close friends. A lot of them got to Cooper Union. They got to good schools. They all went into something related to the arts, except one guy who has a tuxedo-lending outfit. I don't know how that happened.

How did I develop creativity in my classes? I don't know the exact answer to that. But I would say you saw these little kids and you had a lot of feeling for them. And you wanted the kids to live, to have a good life. So you encouraged them: "Don't be afraid, kids. If you think you'd like to build this or that, if we can find a way, we'll build it." You see, I had no curriculum that guided me or told me what I had to do for them. So pretty much you tried to find out organically what they were hungry for. And I think at that time, and often since, I would have taken an approach that was even less creative if it were more humane. I loved my kids. I didn't want anything to hurt them. And to me, the creative factor was that the kid was discovering something, he was growing. In other words, creativity with the human creature, rather than with the paints. The kids would say, "The old man doesn't care what we do with the paints, he doesn't even care if we paint noodles." When they grew to adolescence, they'd want to make nude statues. "All right," I'd say, "but make it here with me, in the shop, don't go around making it on the storefront." It was a kind of permissiveness and a kind of coaching, rather than teaching. You were coaching these kids to try to be something. Also, you trusted them because that's the way they learned to be trusting. They never let me down. I trusted them and they were entirely trustworthy. They still are.

If we had it to do over again, I would like to see a project, but with people younger than I was. I was 21 years old when I went on it. I'd like to see it with boys and girls who are younger, but planned in such a way that it's not busy work, so that it will affect their lives. That's how I got involved. The WPA gave me a chance to teach and for the next 43 years I taught my heart out. I think rather than give people just leaf-raking or busy work, we should take youngsters who have dreams, who want to be something, and start them somewhere in that direction. Put a kid to work in a hospital if that's what he wants, put him to work in a theater where his dreams are, try to help him to realize those dreams. That is a mighty hard process.

Citizenship Schools

That's how the Civil Rights movement began—from Esau Jenkins's bus. Learning to vote was what it was all about. The Highlander Folk School was where it became organized. Other people and other parts of the community started asking for it. Their lives changed.

DOROTHY COTTON • How might I recreate for you the mood, or the atmosphere, out of which our program, the Citizenship Education Program, came into being. How might I bring it alive again for those of you who don't have much knowledge of what went on in that part of the country—in the Bible Belt, as some people called it—some 20 years ago. I thought some of you might not be absolutely sure of what it is we're talking about when we talk about the kind of learning that took place. And I thought maybe a song would help it make more sense, a song we used to sing:

> I been in the storm so long,
> I been in the storm so long children,
> I been in the storm so long,
> Gimme little time to pray.
> Oh, let me tell you sister, just how I come along,
> Gimme little time to pray.
> With a hunger and an aching heart, Lord,
> Gimme a little time to pray.
> I been in the storm so long,
> I been in the storm so long children,
> I been in the storm so long,
> Gimme little time to pray.

Those lines were about the people who came to our program—people who worked in the fields, who picked long rows of cotton "from can to can't," as someone said. I remember a woman singing in a Citizenship Education session one day—and she knew that if she didn't get down that long row, she was going to miss some of the $2.50 or $3.50 a day that she was paid:

> Oh, Lord, I can't make out my row,
> Lord, I can't make out my row,
> And the sun is going down.

Those people were feeling really low, really down. And so they suffered and sang those mournful songs right out of their very lives. And what were they singing about, aching about? Septima Clark, who helped develop and worked with this program, along with the daddy of the program, Myles Horton, told me about a young black man who ran over a dog, a white man's dog, on one of the islands, Johns Island, off the coast of Charleston, South Carolina, and was shot by the dog's owner. The man's family was so intimidated by white folks, and by their whole life situation, that they couldn't bring themselves to protest too loudly. They just cried and moaned about it and made some pitiful attempts to do something about it. I think that really lays down for us the state of the people that we started to work with.

The people were so intimidated that they were afraid to protest. They lived in situations where sometimes there was no time to go to school, and no money to go to school, and poor schools if there were any at all. Mrs. Clark remembers days on Johns Island, where she taught, when the owner of the plantation could knock on the side of that little wooden schoolroom, and all of the poor black children had to run out because it was time to go pick cotton. Nobody gave a damn about whether those kids learned or not. They would knock on the side of the building and out came all of those children, little black children, going to pick cotton. Bad situations. Education was the lowest rung on the ladder, in terms of values for the people, especially if it was education for the disinherited people of the area. Poor schools, bad streets. Can you imagine living in a neighborhood where the streets are paved and suddenly the pavement ends. Well, we know who lives beyond the pavement, it was the black folk and the poor folk. Nobody cared whether their streets were like washboards or not—hardly passable if a hard rain came.

I don't know how I can better help you see and feel what their lives were like. Can you imagine working on a farm and never seeing any money, where everything you bought came from the man at the store, so that at the end of the year, when he would add it up, you could hear him say, "I'm sorry, you didn't make anything this year. In fact, you owe us some money." And you worked in the fields row upon row from can to can't. I once asked a woman what she meant by that, "from can to can't," and she said, "From the time you can see until the time you can't."

We learned a lot in the Citizenship Education Program. People there usually got none of the good jobs, and if they did get one, of course they were the last hired and the first who were fired. They were totally out of the mainstream of life in the community.

I wish I could say to you, with respect to the changes that took place during the decade of the 1960s, that they emanated from the Ivy League schools. I wish I could say to you that they came from the halls of Yale and Harvard and Vassar and City College, but they really did not. The changes that happened during that period happened because people like Myles Horton and Septima Clark and Esau Jenkins decided that these ordinary people really could take over their lives, they really could be in charge of their lives, there was a way for somebody to help them to see that.

Esau, Septima and Myles talked about it one day. Esau said: "You know, if these folks could learn to register to vote, they could change their lot in life." Esau, who operated some buses, taking people back and forth to work from Johns Island to Charleston, decided he was going to start teaching these people how to register to vote. If they voted, he reasoned, they could change things, things would be better, they'd be respected. And so he had Myles place application forms for voter registration on the front of the bus. You had to answer a lot of questions to register to vote in those days. Well, we know that the questions on the application were designed specifically to keep black people and poor people from registering to vote, to keep them out of the political process. The powers that be knew that if the poor participated in the political process, they couldn't treat them unfairly anymore. If they realize that they can control their lives, the people in power said, we can't be in charge; we can't have all the money and the best streets and the best food and rule the people. They knew the power of the ballot. So did Esau Jenkins, Myles Horton, Septima Clark and Richard Robinson, and they started to do something about it.

Esau started teaching the people, on the bus, about the word "vote," and about the Civil Rights Bill. "This is your application," he'd say to them on the bus, "and this is the question you have to answer." And Myles, who was already at the Highlander Folk School, welcomed these people there to further develop that program. The program was a way to teach these people how they could be in charge of their lives, teach them—the way Andrew Young put it—to be free. The idea was to bring them to a workshop, so they could go back into their own communities and teach other people.

That's how the Civil Rights movement began—from Esau Jenkins's bus. Learning to vote was what it was all about. The Highlander Folk School was where it became organized. Other people and other parts of the community started asking for it. Their lives changed. After those workshops, some of the people on those islands were a different kind of people, their communities started to look different. They weren't feeling so oppressed any more. They were still down but not out. They knew that they could now do something about it. They had a sense of hope, at last, with this kind of training, and hope is contagious. And so it spread from the centers of the communities affected to other cities and other towns, and eventually all around the South.

We could talk for days and days and days about the history of the Citizenship Education Program, but instead let me try to summarize it. The powers that be didn't like what Myles and Dick were doing at Highlander; they found all kinds of ways to harass them, and finally closed them down, closed down that beautiful place that was doing so many marvelous things for people. But instead of that marvelous work ending it was taken on by the Southern Christian Leadership Conference, Martin Luther King's organization, and we proceeded to work further. Septima Clark, who worked with the program at Highlander Folk School, came along with it to SCLC and that's where I came in, as director.

People were begging for the program, they were clamoring for it. "Can we go to one of your Citizenship Education classes?" they asked. And we wanted to spread the word. We looked for more money. For a time people were pouring money into the program. People knew that this was what was needed and they wanted to help. Septima Clark, Andrew Young, who is now in the United States Congress, and I would get in our cars and drive all over the South telling people about the Citizenship Education Program. We would talk to anybody in town that showed any leadership potential. It could be the preacher, it could be the president of a civic group, it could be the undertaker down the street. There were natural leaders in every neighborhood. We would seek out these people and ask them to come away with us—to come into their natural leadership a little more fully, and to work in some of the ways that would bring about basic changes in their lives. And they came—50, 60, sometimes 70 at a time, to stay together in a five-day residential workshop. That went on for maybe 10, 11, 12, or 13 years. I'm not exactly sure what the time was, in terms of that phase of the work.

What happened in these sessions? Maybe you know the name of Fanny Hamer. Mrs. Hamer was on one of the buses that came to the program from Broomfield, Mississippi. With the aid of money from a foundation, we could charter a bus very often and bring busloads from whole communities. Think of what could happen if a group of people from one community was exposed to some of this beautiful stuff, a whole busload, that could go back and spread themselves around the community and begin to work toward some of the changes that were brought about on Johns Island. That is exactly what happened.

Fanny Lou Hamer came to one of our workshops, from Mr. Marlowe's plantation in Broomfield, Mississippi, a plantation where she'd been run off for trying to talk somebody into coming. Mrs. Hamer said her husband had been told he would be killed and they would be kicked out of the house, if she didn't stop that voter registration work she was doing around there. And she did, in fact, go away to another city in Mississippi. But one day she called her husband and said, "Would you please come and get me, I can't run any more." That was my first knowing of Mrs. Hamer. In the opening session of that workshop, she sang some of the songs that I was singing a minute ago. And we went from the getting-to-know-you session, finding out where people were in terms of their feelings and how they saw things, to, well, let me jump across a good number of years. Picture, if you will, that Mrs. Hamer, standing up at the National Democratic Convention, contending with Mississippi Senator Eastland and the delegates there, saying, "This delegation, sir, ladies and gentlemen, is seated illegally because black folks are disenfranchised in Mississippi. This is the legitimate delegation here."

I'm saying that the Citizenship Education Program helped Mrs. Hamer go from that Mr. Marlowe's plantation, singing those sorrowful songs, to standing up at that convention, saying, "We won't take it any more." Classic example of one of the graduates, if you will, of that program.

What happened in the sessions? Sometimes we made an outline. The outlines were of basic documents. People who were going to struggle for their rights ought to know something about the country's basic documents. And people learned how to read and write. The people of Johns Island couldn't read and write, so how were they going to understand this complicated application to register and vote. As a matter of fact, sometimes we told people that it was a literacy program. But you know what they were taught instead: "Vote for your country. Do you know what that means? This word spells 'mayor.' Who is yours? How'd he get there?" And we'd talk about it for hours. And people came into a new realization about themselves. We would walk into a class where basic documents were being outlined and ask them, "Now, what are you going to do with that?" They needed to know some things about the Constitution.

As Septima Clark said about some of the folks who came, now knowing how to read or write: "They may have a third-grade education, but they had Ph.D. minds." And they did indeed. So we would say to them: "What's a citizen? What's a citizen?" "O.K.," they would say back, "I've thought about that for a long time and I'd like to work that out with you." They would say you're a citizen if "you register to vote, or if you went to church regularly, or if you paid your taxes, or if you"—we got all kinds of answers. And we got good arguments about what a citizen was. And in the process we were writing away, you know, working away. This is a "c," and this is an "i," and this is a "t," and an "i," and that's a "z," but what is a "citizen?" And eventually we'd put some answers together and decide—the group would decide: "Any one born in this country is a citizen." We might work for hours on the word "citizen," and then apply what we had learned to this thing called "the Constitution." "What is that other good 'c' word?" we'd ask. "Right, Constitution. C-o-n-...." They had to learn to read and write the Constitution. And the Constitution had something called—a good "a" word—amendments. An "a," and "m," and "e," and "n,"—"Amendment." "Then there is the 14th Amendment," we would say, "and the 14th Amendment says, 'All citizens born or naturalized in the United States are citizens of the United States.' And it also says, 'Nothing can make it a law that takes away your privileges.' " And we could work with that sentence right there for a whole day. And, therefore, we would say, "You who just came from Selma, Alabama, where George Wallace is telling you that you can't march down highway A to protest the fact that you cannot register to vote—well, you know now that this basic document here, the Constitution of the United States, says that you can. What is that Constitution?" And after another half-hour of discussion, somehow we put together, right out of the group, that the Constitution was the supreme law of the land. "Well, if that's the supreme law of the land and no state can make a law to take away your privileges, then what do you do about it?" "Wow, then Mr. Wallace can't tell me that I can't march, because the First Amendment tells me I *do* have rights to gather and to petition for redress of my grievances." And people who couldn't read and write would come away from sessions like that knowing more about citizenship than I ever learned in anybody's college, and I have been to many of them.

And I tell you that we eventually had really heterogeneous grouping, ranging from people like Mrs. Hamer from Mr. Marlowe's plantation, to, at one time, a whole graduate class from Putney, Vermont, which sat, all 11 of them, in one class for a whole week. And they said it, too: They learned from those people who came from plantations, who were making this thing come alive. And there were other people—they called themselves by many names, from nationalist to whatever; you name it—who came to a new realization here of who they were and what their place really could be. Some of them, on the first day, said: "What are you people doing here talking about the Constitution? We know about Revolution, we know what needs to be done." They were going to lead the people, in spite of the fact that the people couldn't read and write and register and make demands for themselves. And then on the second day, they realized they were really just screaming. They really needed to learn what the thing was about, and how to move; they needed to learn how to organize people. And so that happened there. These people went back home to teach, they went back home to organize their community. They were asked to set up Citizenship Education Clubs, and they did, and the clubs sprung up all over the South. They would come to our workshops on a regular basis and then transmit some of this new sense of their own survival to the people in their own communities, who hadn't had the opportunity of sitting in some of the sessions with us.

Sometimes people would come and sit there complaining, moaning about how the welfare office or the unemployment office treats them so bad. And after a few minutes of talking about how bad that is, we'd raise a question, like: "You know this and you know this. Well, why don't you go and be the welfare lady?" There would be a silence. "Why don't you be the unemployment clerk?" Or, "Why don't you tell the unemployment clerk what your rights are?" They were so down and out that they had never realized, "Hey, I could do that, too." But in the end, they would say, "I'm going home and I'm not going to take that scene any more." And we did it, they did it, we all did it. We showed the people in the small communities that you really can work there, in that place, the courthouse. It doesn't have to be that place where black folk get beat up every Saturday night, or get intimidated, or harassed. We had to move the feeling of oppressed people so they could see that, and they saw that, and the symbols of oppression, and brutality, and intimidation, and harassment were vanquished. Now you can see black folks sitting at the courthouse and working there. And so that was leadership training.

As I said before, I wish I could say that all of these great changes during the struggle of the 1960s, and they were important, emanated from the halls of the Ivy League schools. But I tell you that the changes emanated from those people who sat in those sessions, who were from those plantations, and who went back home and said, "We ain't going to take it no more." I know that isn't grammatical, but that's all right. When they said, "I ain't gonna take it no more," I heard that with tears in my eyes.

One day, when I looked behind me in a church, in one of those forgotten neighborhoods, to see an old black woman—you know, face all wrinkled and hands all gnarled—one could just see the whole history of a suffering people in her face; there was suffering there, yet there was hope, and the church was rocking; we always sang, somehow that kept us together, it kept the spirit up—and so to look at that woman's face, and hear her voice, with the church going, everyone singing:

> I ain't going to let nobody turn me 'round,
> Turn me 'round, turn me 'round;
> Ain't going to let nobody turn me 'round,
> Keep on awalkin',
> Keep on atalkin',
> Marching up to freedom land.
> Ain't going to let George Wallace turn me 'round,
> Turn me 'round,
> Ain't going to let them turn me 'round,
> Ain't goin' to let George Wallace turn me 'round,
> Goin' to keep on a walkin', keep on a talkin',
> Walking up to freedom land.

And she knew it. I cried watching her sing. And I cried seeing her walking with a picket sign.

MYLES HORTON • Dorothy Cotton mentioned Esau Jenkins. Esau not only was the one who asked for this program at the Citizenship School, as it came to be called, but he started his own center on Johns Island. We helped him to get money to build his own center and start programs there. And sometimes we'd run our own programs there on Johns Island. But Esau's center wasn't part of Highlander. He was on our board and we worked together, but his center was independent. There'd be other places that had centers and they would be independent, too. Highlander was one of its kind in the hearts and minds of people everywhere; it had a physical base, but its spirit wasn't limited to a building or a program.

Nobody knew who was Highlander or who wasn't. I would be down in Mississippi and some woman would come up to me and say, "Who are you?" And I'd say, and then she'd say, "Where you from?" And I'd say, and then she'd say, "You know, I'm a teacher at Highlander." And I'd look at her, you know. And she'd say, "Did you ever hear of Highlander?" And I'd say, "Yeah." And she'd say, "I'm a Citizenship School teacher." And I said, "Yeah, I know something about them. She said, "Did you ever teach one?" And I said, "No, no, black folks teach Citizenship Schools." And she said, "That's right." But was I interested in them? And I said, "Where did you get to be a Citizenship School teacher?" And she said that she had gone to somebody else's Citizenship School in Mississippi—somebody who had learned something about voting— and then started her own Citizenship School and certified herself as a teacher. And that was done all over the country: people would make up their minds they were going to run a school and they'd run a school. Now that tells you something about the history of this idea.

When we first started these sessions, we didn't call it a school. I am so anti-schooling that I didn't like the idea of schools or teachers or any kind of thing like that. I only believed in education. Those other things get in the way. So I said, "Let's pick a name for this, just any kind of name." And they said, "It's a school." I've learned that when anyone says it's a school, it's a school. If they said it's a school, it's okay with me, it's a school. And then I said, "Well, it's not going to be a regular school with teachers, and so on, is it? What kind of school is it going to be?" Some people began to call it a Literacy School, others called it an Adult School, others a Night School, and things like that. And then some folks suggested Citizenship School. And I said, "Why is it a citizenship school?" And they said, "We want to make us first-class citizens. This is going to be school to make us first-class citizens!"

So the black people of Johns Island, who couldn't read and write, named them Citizenship Schools. They named them, the name didn't come from us. About all we did was to say it would be informal, there would be no restrictions of any kind. It had to be a challenging goal, something really to stretch people and make them work hard for citizenship or voting or civil rights or something like that. But there wouldn't be any educators, any trained teachers, in the program. They were prohibited by us; nobody who was a trained teacher could teach at a Citizenship School. Anybody who had any kind of training would have to make it so structured and so step-by-stepish that the adults wouldn't stay and wouldn't come back. You had to avoid anything like that. Even though they named it 'school' and called themselves 'teacher,' they had to be very careful to see to it that it was the people who were the teachers in those schools and who were kind of their peers, careful so that they wouldn't be too structured and wouldn't impose ideas on the people who came, because it was good for them, but would respond to them. Above all, Citizenship School teachers would have to have solidarity with people, they would have to be free of being judgmental. So we were very careful to keep teachers out of this thing. As long as Highlander operated the program—we ran it I think for three or four years—we never got any teachers to teach. We wanted education to take place—so we kept trained teachers out.

The first 'teacher' in the program was Bernice Robinson, who was a seamstress and a beautician, who had been to Highlander and in a moment of weakness, once, said, "Anything I could ever do for Highlander, I'd like to do it." I asked her if she wanted to teach at the school and she said, "Oh, no; I can't do that." I reminded her of what she had said. She said, "I didn't mean it, you know," but she gave in anyway. And she didn't know a thing about it. Septima Clark was there; she was on the staff—she's a black woman who got fired from the Charleston, South Carolina, school system for joining the NAACP, I think, or coming to Highlander. And Septima tried to help Bernice by offering her some old charts—she'd worked in a literacy program in the Second World War. But Bernice didn't need anything. She pasted the United Nations' Declaration of Human Rights on the wall, as well as Highlander's statement of principles, and the Constitution, which they had to learn to read. Anyway, she started out challenging the people. They were adults; they were men and women. They'd break pencils. They'd hold them so hard, they'd break them. They were used to holding a shovel or a plow, not pencils. But those people learned how to read in that first Citizenship School.

The people had to agree to come for two nights a week for three months. We fixed up a room in the back of Esau's store, put paper on the walls, and had a potbellied stove going in the wintertime. They started out with 18 people and ended up with 30. And over 80 percent of the people in that time— two nights a week—learned; they graduated. The criterion for graduation was if they could register and vote. If they registered, got the registration certificate, that meant they'd learned to read well enough to pass the test, and they graduated. That's the only exam we had because that's what it was all about.

I'm from South Carolina, a place called Andersonville, and I remember that first Sunday we heard about the Citizenship School. They announced it in all the churches. They were going to have a voters' meeting, they called it, and everybody was asked to come. And it was like a whole day, a whole Sunday afternoon of talking, and talking about what your lives were, and getting organized, and that kind of thing. And it really turned out to be one of the best things that ever happened to such a small, small town, because now they still hold meetings in the church, something like once a month, and that's where they bring all the grievances they have. They have somebody on the City Council now and they go through the whole thing. The program really has been beneficial.

COTTON ● Well, you know, as far as I'm concerned, it all started back then. Towns would come together just that way. They'd start talking around that little potbellied stove there about what their rights were. And they'd come to a real resolution that "We're not going to take it."

HORTON ● I'll tell you another thing, if you can understand it. People always draw up grand detailed plans; they make all kinds of analyses. Well, that's a good way not to do anything. If you really are serious, then you do just one thing, do it well, and let it spread on its merits. And if it can't spread on its merits, it's never going to spread. How many plans never make it! We never promoted anything. We always refused to promote. If the people don't want to peddle it, it's no good. We were concerned with one simple thing. We spent six months getting ready, seeing if we could do it, analyzing it, making sure it was a success, as far as you can in your mind. We were going to do it one time, win or lose. And we didn't want to experiment on people.

It's a terrible thing to experiment on people. You have to learn by experience, but how I rationalize that is by setting it up so that the people themselves are involved, and learn from their experience. Even if you lose but learn from your losing, then you win because you've learned something. I guess a better name for it is "action research." So we set it up so that it was the people's from the beginning. They named it. They ran it. It was theirs, and if it was going to fail then they would know why it was failing, and analyze it, and then come out of the ashes and do something. We shot the works, one time.

Word spreads by mouth very fast. Whoever's been poor knows that poor people don't trust anything that isn't spoken word, and they don't trust all that. But that's the way things move. So when word spread that 80 percent of these people had been to the Citizenship School and registered to vote, they started bragging about it, as people will and should. We're citizens, they'd say, and we're going to vote. That word spread, and people from other parts of Johns Island came and said, "Look, can we have one of those schools?" And then pretty soon, people came from other islands, all up and down the coast; they started island jumping. And then after six months of that, it started jumping from state to state. And we never did anything. We just let it spread of its own accord. It was the grapevine.

It got to the place where somebody would come to us and say, "We'd like to have a Citizenship School," and we'd say, "Well, do you know what's involved?" "No," they'd say, "but we'd like to have one like they have on Johns Island." And I'd say, "Well, what's involved here is this: Highlander will pay for pencils and paper; the rest of the money we have to raise somehow." I worked out the costs once with Martin (Luther King). I think it was around $30 per person to train. Most programs in the world cost $30,000 per person. But we didn't have any ways to spend any more money than that. And we said we'd do that. And they said, "Well, how about a teacher?" And we'd say, "Anybody that wants to be a teacher in this—local people, that is, not a regular teacher—anybody who is interested in voting and wants to do it, could be a teacher and could organize a school." Or if two people worked together and they wanted to organize a school, then they could get a teacher. It's easy; it works either way. Highlander would come in and make it possible; then we'd just walk off, and leave it with them.

We took the teachers who had kind of selected themselves and been selected; none of them were teachers in the professional sense. All of them were teachers in the real sense of education. Some of them could hardly read and write, but as I said, that wasn't important. It was scarcely important when you could get technicians to do things like read and write. We took four or five of the most vocal people, who could talk to other people, and weren't too shy, and we made them the teachers: that was the faculty of the Citizenship Schools. From the time we took on Bernice Robinson, who taught that first Citizenship School, all the teachers were from the inside. That's the pattern that was set up. That's how the thing grew. And she grew to the place where we had thousands of people. It went sky high. Got too big for us. We were glad to get rid of the damn thing. There was too much for us to handle. Once a thing like that starts moving, it's time to start something else.

Someone asked before how we could cover the amount of material we said we did. Well, you know, it really doesn't take long if you can't register to vote, and you don't have anything to eat, and your son is getting beat up every night by somebody who's decided they'll use a broom on people; it doesn't take you long to understand that there's a document that says that can't happen. You can learn that in 15 minutes.

We used to have to hide out sometimes. We'd have to put out the lights, and whisper. You'd go on, and then later on you'd get the lights going again, when it was safe. Or you might crawl out the back door and just keep crawling. You'd come back, though. People never got discouraged; they never quit. They just kept learning.

COTTON • "Are there Citizenship classes going on now?" I'm really not sure how to answer that. We were together for five minutes the other week to ask ourselves the same question: "Where is the movement now?" Insofar as there was a certain cadre of people who came together—who formed a network that spread out to Citizenship Schools and other things—we all were part of the movement. Well, that same network is still doing its thing, but not in the same structure. I have a feeling that much of what I learned in Highlander and in the Citizenship Education Program is what I'm still doing as Director of a Head Start program. In other words, we're still working. Some people are very much concerned that there is not a "leader" and an "organization," both of which are focused on a single issue, but I think there's still a movement.

HORTON • It's going on, but it's taking another form. I know, literally, hundreds of people who are doing things in their own way, who came out of the movement. Some are in politics, some are in cooperatives, some are in education. They are using all kinds of things and a lot of the ideas that they learned in the movement, expressing it in a different form. In that respect, you could say the movement is going on. But the other thing that is happening, that I've seen, and it bothers me, is that it isn't reaching down and out to new people, as it did at one time. At one time it was so contagious, you almost had to have a feeling if you got within 10 miles of somebody. Kids would run and tell everyone. The word did spread. There was a contagion there. Out of that movement came great creativity and people extended themselves; they did things they couldn't do. They did the impossible thing all the time.

That was the beauty of the movement—reaching out and getting to the real core, getting to the people who couldn't read or write, getting to people who had been off a plantation maybe once or twice in their lives. People to whom the "government" meant the deputy sheriff. That was the only government they'd ever known. And then they knew that at the receiving end of clubs. The movement reached people who'd come out to start a Citizenship School or who had come out to register to vote or to do things. In Mississippi, the Head Start program was taking over at that time, so they'd run a Head Start program. They were doing it. And that spread. Now, it seems to me, that has stopped and it's left a tremendous lot of poor people behind who are not being directly involved. To me, that's a real loss. Not that people who are in it aren't doing something, but it's not continuing to spread. The dynamic of it is stopped. People got to start getting stirred again.

I grew up in a poor mountain family, essentially religious but not overly. Accepted everything, all the social structures, not knowing any better. But I don't think I was ever mean; my parents were never mean. I think I was in college before I ever thought about the fact that there were privileges growing out of being white or out of being rich. Privileges that grow out of economics or color or race or religion. And then it began to dawn on me that I wasn't as privileged as a lot of people, that, in fact, I was poor; I had to work all the time. I started to make a living when I was 14, and a lot of children didn't have to do that. I found out there was a difference. Some people were going to school and didn't have to work; they weren't even very smart. I wasn't very smart either, but I was serious. They weren't serious. When I was in high school, I never heard much music, unless somebody'd come and play the violin or they'd have a concert. And I never could *go* to those things; I never had the quarter. I had to stand outside and listen. But I found that a lot of people were outside, not inside.

I learned a lot of things as I went along. Things weren't quite right. I wasn't hurt personally, because I was doing fine, myself. I was having a good time and making it all right. I had a lot of friends and wasn't taking life too seriously. But then, when I wanted certain things—and for reasons which I don't know about—I concluded that I had no right to anything that everybody else didn't have a right to. In other words, if I wanted something, I'd have to want it for you as well as for me. And I think that was kind of a beginning of an interest and an understanding, of identifying, with people in poverty.

Dewey's Synthesis: Science and Feeling

JOSEPH FEATHERSTONE ● This conference has been put together partly to honor the figures in the past who have been working in a genuine tradition. We need to know that there is an educational tradition to draw on. Often this is something we forget. Sometimes I think of this country as the United States of Amnesia. Particularly in debates over education, we seem doomed to keep repeating ancient ritual battles between the old and the new. We seem to be stuck on a pendulum that swings between mindless slogans of freedom and equally mindless slogans called authority, the three Rs, or law and order, and so on. In part, this reflects the fact that we're not very conscious of the past, so we lack perspective on the present. We don't know where we can build on past traditions in useful ways, ways that would make for a cumulative set of gains for schools and other institutions, a spiral, rather than a pendulum. Nor do we know where we must break away from the past completely and strike out in wholly new directions. Today, I want to talk about an issue that John Dewey struggled with and that we still struggle with today. It is central to the dilemmas raised by the second round of the New Education in the last 80 years of American history. It is the issue of romanticism.

Both the hopes of romanticism and the irrationalities of romanticism are central to what has been good and bad in the New Education. What do I mean by romanticism? Romanticism conjures up many things. It conjures up good things: aspirations for life, a freedom from restraint, a kind of completeness and harmony of vision. It also conjures up sad things. "Romantic" can mean the irrational, the sentimental, the nostalgic. Our culture is deeply romantic in both senses. We have never fully come to terms with romanticism, being relatively ignorant of the past in the United States of Amnesia—and we keep shifting around between romantic hopes for education and children and romantic illusions about that.

In one way or another, the issue of romanticism hovers in the background of John Dewey's efforts to think more clearly about school reform. It may sound strange to think of Dewey as involved with romanticism. Dewey was, after all, a pragmatist, a dissenter from the reigning American romantic traditions. In what I think of as his Progressive phase—roughly up to the 1920s—Dewey wanted to put science at the center of American life. I should explain what I mean by the word "progressive." When we say "progressive" in education we usually mean child-centered education. Yet historians use the word "progressive" to describe the entire intellectual generation that came of age between, roughly, 1880 and 1920. "Progressive education" thus embraces all facets of this generation's concerns with education—the whole attempt to reshape the schools in the name of science, psychology, and democracy. Mainstream progressive education was enormously influenced by testing and the application of "science to schools." The progressive educators we think of—the child-centered wing—were actually a small, but influential minority. In many ways, the progressive Dewey is a scientistic figure, who tends to emphasize science at the expense of other realms. This is particularly striking, in fact, in his educational thinking where, as a progressive, Dewey is actually quite hostile to the imagination, the use of art, for example. Dewey shifted his emphasis late in his life. It is fascinating to follow the changes in his thinking in the period after World War I, especially in the 1920s and 1930s. In many ways the later Dewey tries to transcend the bleak and rather managerial scientism of so much of the mainstream progressive outlook.

For a time, in the middle part of his career, Dewey looked like the spokesman for a new order of professionals—managers and school reformers—bent on rationalizing American life, putting it on a scientific and corporate basis. In reading this Dewey today, we are still enormously impressed by the pedagogy, impressed by what he has to say about psychology and children's minds, and yet put off, in a way, by the naive faith in technology—in science and progress—which was such a characteristic part of the mainstream progressive thought. Late in his life, however, in the 1920s and 1930s, at an age when many of us have retired, Dewey began writing what I think of as his masterpieces. Harold Bloom has suggested that every new attempt to go beyond romanticism has ended up with the fresh realization of the priority of romanticism. Dewey's commitment to science, and his pragmatism, had been a major break with romantic American philosophical and literary traditions. Nonetheless, the late work finds Dewey exploring many of the themes of the Romantics, especially the romanticism of what F. O. Matthiessen called the "American Renaissance" of Walt Whitman and Emerson. As a scientific mind, Dewey had always been clear that Emerson was wrong to think that there were truths of the heart as well as truths of the head. In Dewey's scientific world, there was only one kind of truth: the kind you got through the scientific method. And yet the late Dewey was much more clear, as he put it, that life is not mainly a cognitive affair. In books like *Art as Experience*—one of my favorite books and one that I wish teachers would read with Dewey's other educational books—Dewey is a scientific mind hoping to establish portions of what I call the high romantic synthesis of science and feeling on a new, more modestly empirical footing.

Dewey's high romantic ambitions have not been evident to most of his readers because of the centrality of his commitments to science. And, of course, the dreary matter-of-factness of his style—which some people have compared to sculpting with peanut butter—didn't help. Nobody was less of a romantic by temperament than John Dewey; he was what William James would have called "a healthy-minded soul," healthy-minded perhaps to a fault. Yet he was working to repair Emerson's fleeting high romantic synthesis of science and feeling. This is central to understanding his educational ambitions and the rest of his philosophy.

All the different varieties of romanticism—a man named Lovejoy once counted 13 of them—are protests on behalf of the organic and the concrete against the mechanistic and the abstract. This is true in education and in other realms. There is high romanticism and there is low romanticism. Those of us who have lived through the countercultural revolts of the 1960s will know what I mean by low romanticism. In education and other realms, what I call low romanticism exalts the heart over the head, celebrating the irrational and the intuitive, and shrinking away defensively from science and reason. Mainly low romanticism exalts instinct and fears rationality. In some ways, as Dewey well knew—this was part of his scientific rage at the low romanticism of the 19th century—low romanticism has been the dominant American literary and philosophical tradition. In a sense, low romanticism was what Dewey was rebelling against: sentimentality, subjectivity, nostalgia; the foolish side of romanticism. High romanticism, on the other hand, is the recurring search for a saving middle way between the cold icy reductions of analytic science and the undisciplined craziness of the solitary romantic ego. High romanticism welcomes science and reason within their proper domains. Its enemies are irrationality on the one hand and scientism on the other—scientism being all the partial and limited modes of scientific thought that deny the power and autonomy of the human imagination and falsely claim to render a complete account of experience. High romanticism is an ideal of reason reinforced by feeling. It is a quest for a middle way, in which reason reinforces feeling in the exercise of the imagination. It is what a high romantic poet, Wallace Stevens, calls "reasoning with a later reason."

Dewey attacked Emerson's dualistic universe that divided the truths of the head from the truths of the heart. But Dewey was Emerson's heir in trying to mediate the instrumental abstractions of science and the values inherent in concrete experience, to fuse science and meaning. Dewey's late works such as *Experience and Nature* and *Art as Experience* are efforts both to transcend romanticism and to preserve its deepest insights. Central to this for Dewey is his discovery of art late in his life. He met a man named Barnes, who had discovered Argyrol and had a beautiful art collection, a complex crazy figure; Barnes was a big influence on Dewey. Dewey's discovery of art was an effort to escape the scientism, the brittle, dry, rationalistic and rather self-conscious progressive cast of thought. Certainly it had been necessary in a scientific age to go beyond Emerson's often crazy romantic subjectivity. But, science alone, analysis alone, was also inadequate. Abstraction and self-consciousness had to be overcome or the result would be dessication and what the Romantics had feared all along as death-in-life. Another way to put this is to say Dewey was looking for a way to frame intuition and the imagination within certain consciously created limits. In art, he found the example and the metaphor for the controlled liberation of intuition he had been looking for.

As I say, Dewey's basic educational ideas had been laid out in his middle, Progressive years. Reading the late Dewey, however, and particularly the Dewey of *Art as Experience*, you get a much richer picture of what he had in mind for children. David Hawkins, in a recent collection of essays, *The Informed Vision*, calls it a style of education that begins in play and evolves into apprenticeship, an education that teaches children both a reverence for concrete esthetic experience and a mastery of the proper place of symbols and abstractions in a scientific universe. The ideal was a soberly chastened, empirical version of the high romantic synthesis.

It's very interesting that when Americans get around to writing their autobiographies—Dewey never did—they think of life as an education: Ben Franklin's life, Lincoln Steffens's life, are "educations." Even Henry Adams thought of his life as an ironic education in the extent to which he had been miseducated for dealing with a modern universe. I think of Dewey's life as a kind of education. Seeing life as an education is a mark of a recurring American earnestness and optimism that says it always remains possible to grow and learn in the present, whatever the odds in the present and whatever the past defeats. Part of Dewey's education was a never altogether finished set of lessons on the limits of past American reform traditions. In some ways, Dewey was a little bit like an innocent hero in a Henry James story trying to save some healing vestiges of his innocence as he wanders further and further into the world's dark labyrinths.

The late Dewey learned a lot. After World War I, he had shed the progressive illusion of progress. He also learned that his true vocation was not so much as a progressive social engineer but as a radical social critic who was much clearer on the chasms between what his hopes were for American society and what the realities of that culture were. He learned, too, about the chasm between mainstream progressive educational reform, which was so heavily administrative and managerial in its emphases, and his own child-centered brand of progressive education: He learned that history was not inevitably on the side of the child-centeredness. But he didn't give up; he persisted.

In the long run, the child-centered progressives like Dewey opened debates that are still going on, and which, of course, include a good deal more than just schooling in this culture. The child-centered progressives started by insisting on the intellectual and educational significance of play and on the importance of styles of teaching that moved children from play to more disciplined work. They felt that the present lives of children ought to have as much of a claim on educators' attention as their futures, that, in a much abused but still valid phrase, "school was life, as well as preparation for life." Against the historically conformist grain of American schooling, which had been in large part a story of culture factories and school machines, they emphasized children's diversity and uniqueness, and the fact that childhood is above all a time of construction, a time in which children actively forge the structures of thought out of their varied encounters with experience. Most profoundly, the child-centered progressives broke with mainstream progressive thought in rejecting the mainly economic view of education that evolved in the progressive era, the educational outlook that looked to schools to serve corporate and managerial ends. If there was always an essential vagueness to Dewey's critique, it was an important critique nevertheless. He was making a point that has often been made since with even less coherence: namely, that capitalist industrial America needed a more communal perspective, more communal values, more communal institutions.

But when we think of the grandness and sweep of something like Dewey's attempt to do a high romantic synthesis—to blend science and feeling—and what that would entail in education, we have to see Dewey as a utopian, in both the good and bad senses of the word. Utopian in the bad sense in that very often Dewey articulated visions without being clear about strategies for getting to at least within sight of the vision. The optimistic, progressive Dewey was quite mistaken to think that schools could be the main engine of social reform. He thought he had shown how schools alone could transform society, when actually all he had shown was some of the pre-conditions for decent schools—which were, of course, in and of themselves very much worth having. Dewey is a utopian in the good sense of the word in that he points the way to what many of us are, in our modest way, working toward. The best child-centered work now, as in the past, is very good. All of us who have been participating in this second round of the New Education feel confident that figures like Fred Hechinger have written premature obituaries on the very lively work that is now going on in many classrooms. For all the budget cuts, the climate of reaction and gloom and despair, the racial turmoil and everything else, many classrooms are still very lively places, indeed. Our schools are a little more tolerant of diverse styles of learning and teaching than they used to be. But the high romantic synthesis has always been unstable, and anyone who speaks about it in education today has to speak with what somebody once called "the authority of failure."

In our own efforts to reformulate reform tradition, as we study the work of progressive educators in the past at this conference today, I think we should try to be very clear, first of all, that there is a past. This is one way of conquering the sense of living in the United States of Amnesia. I would like us to learn of the strengths in our past, the fact that there are examples, that there are heroic people who have done marvelous work, and that these traditions are ongoing. We are part of historic movements with tenacious roots and tenacious aspirations. But also, it is important to study the past of open, progressive, informal, decent—or whatever we want to call it—education to get some sense of its historic weaknesses. Here the issue of romanticism illumines a series of fault lines in a tradition that has often been romantic in the bad as well as the good sense of the word, sentimental about children and sentimental, too, about the constraints society puts on schools.

Finally, it is important to say that going through Dewey's thoughts on these matters, one finds that he's never exactly an answer man. He asks the central questions but doesn't necessarily find the answers. If we approach him or the best practitioners in the past, we will not find answers. What we'll find in the work of the best practitioners, and in Dewey himself, is a kind of completeness of agenda and completeness of vision that ought to be a constant rebuke to the eternal partiality of our insights. The striking thing about Dewey's experimental elementary school was not so much that the work was so wonderful but that, typically, Dewey tried to incorporate all the different elements of what might go into good learning and a good school: a psychology, a curriculum, a sense of the teacher's role—the whole complex thing. Because of the complexity of Dewey's commitments, he's always a reminder to each generation that reinterprets him of what's getting left out. If you haven't got the complete, extraordinarily balanced ticket in education, so to speak, you're missing the point as far as Dewey was concerned.

We struggle with figures like Dewey, too, because in many ways our educational and intellectual agenda for the whole culture was laid out in the Progressive Era. Despite our dazed sense of change and future shock, we have been living in a fairly settled order whose debates have taken fairly traditional forms, debates in education being a notable example of that. The Progressive educational agenda is ours: education as work or preparation for work vs. education for play and intrinsic value; universalism vs. pluralism; equality vs. meritocracy. These remain the great issues. We're apt to write an angry history about progressive reformers mostly—and I don't think I'm being too psychiatric here—because we continue to share their hopes. To ask what Dewey thought about democracy, art, education, romanticism, is to ask what we think about them today. To think about his response to American possibilities is to ask what ours is. This is what makes him such a central figure.

Just before Dewey retired from Columbia, he got a postcard from Texas that had just one sentence on it. It read: "This is just to tell you, Mr. Dewey, that you're going straight to hell." Feelings run high over a figure like Dewey, because the questions he asked, if not the answers he gave, have never been more pertinent.

Some Economic Questions

PAUL NASH ● Open education has been characterized by the development of basic changes in the authority relationships that exist in the teaching-learning situation—from dependence towards independence and, ultimately, towards interdependence. It has been marked by a change from student dependence on the traditional authority figure, the teacher. In open education, the teacher has taken on a different role or function. She has become one who provides what I would call a *liberating structure,* so that the children in the situation can grow in independence and, ultimately, in interdependence. Teachers in open education situations that I've seen are usually better at the former than the latter. That is, they are better at helping children to grow in independence than helping them to grow in interdependence. This is not meant derogatorily. It just happens that the second is much harder and is a much more complex and advanced stage of freedom than independence. It's also bucking some very important trends in the history of the American ethos to move towards interdependence.

We can see immediately one aspect of the nature of open education in America: it has been a rhythmical movement. It rises and falls rhythmically with the rise and the fall of the striving for the attainment of the experience of independence and interdependence. Therefore, the roots of open education in America are very closely tied with the history of democracy in America. I am not a person who believes that the United States is a democratic country. I believe, rather, that it is a very complex country. And in this country there are tendencies toward democracy and tendencies against democracy. I think this is as true today as it has been since the founding of this country. We are always in this condition of tension between these tendencies, and there's never a resting point. But there have been important times in our history when I think we have moved towards democracy. They have been mostly times of affluence and of rising expectations; in other words, the times when people get rich, or—more accurately—when people *feel* rich—and it may be more important to feel rich than to be rich. When people get rich or feel rich, they begin to feel confident. This good feeling about themselves then affects their feelings about other people, especially about children. They are more likely to start trusting children. They assume that children can follow their own natural impulses with some degree of safety. When we mention feelings like that, we immediately identify one of the intellectual roots of open education, which is, of course, romanticism. The romantic root—from Jean-Jacques Rousseau and Pestalozzi and Friedrich Froebel to the transcendentalists and William James and Dewey—is a very important historical thread in the history of open education. In conditions of relaxation, confidence, and affluence, there is a feeling of expansion—a burgeoning of the human spirit. With this burgeoning, people experience less need to control, less need to dominate, less need to predict, less need to guarantee. They become more ready to take risks. Out of a risk-taking attitude come the willingness and the eagerness to structure pedagogical situations where the outcomes are uncertain. There is a trust that the outcomes will be good if children are allowed to participate in acts of discovery, acts of invention, acts of organization, acts of self-management.

On the other hand, when there is no economic margin in life—and this is the case for a lot of people in this country who either *are* poor or, more importantly, *feel* poor—the opposite is true. One becomes withdrawn, tense, tight, suspicious, fearful. A recent article by Urie Bronfenbrenner illustrates this. He writes:

> The frustrations are greatest for the family of poverty, where the capacity for human response is crippled by hunger, cold, filth, sickness, and despair. No parent who spends his days in search of menial work and his nights in keeping the rats away

from the crib can be expected to find the time, let alone the heart, to engage in constructive activities with his children or serve as a stable source of love and discipline. The fact that some beleaguered parents manage to do so is a tribute to them but not to the society in which they live.

For families who can get along, the rats are gone but the rat race remains. The demands of a job, or often two jobs, that claim mealtimes, evenings, and weekends, as well as days, the trips and moves necessary to get ahead or simply hold one's own, the ever-increasing time spent in commuting, parties, evenings out, social and community obligations, all the things that one has to do to meet so-called primary responsibilities, produce a situation in which a child often spends more time with a passive babysitter than a participating parent.

The chief enemy of open education, in other words, is fear. Fear has many allies, one of the most important being inflation. Inflation means working harder this year than last year to stay in the same place. It's not enough to maintain the same salary; you must increase your salary in order to stay at the same economic level. But to increase your salary every year means pleasing someone in authority over you. It means subordinating, perhaps ingratiating, yourself, and developing a whole congeries of attitudes and procedures regarding authority that are the enemies of self-actualization, self-confidence, independence, and interdependence. Therefore, in times of inflation or economic recession, it is very hard, and has been very hard, to nurture open education, because in these times the forces of fear are strengthened. What we get in such times is the consequences of the strengthening of fear. You are familiar with them, as I am, but let me catalogue some of the more obvious ones.

One of the most obvious consequences of an atmosphere of fear is a concern for *boundaries*. Boundary setting often becomes an obsessive activity. For example, there is great concern for the *discipline* of a field. Is this psychology or sociology? Is it history or philosophy? Is it education or therapy? There is concern, often exquisitely defined, with categories and categorization; a concern with unionization and professionalization; a concern with professional licensing and certification; a concern with the development of what George Bernard Shaw called "professions as conspiracies against the laity." There are questions like: Is it schoolwork or is it homework? Is it "A" work or is it "B" work? And so on. You know the dreary list as well as I do.

Open education, on the other hand, means questioning *all* boundaries—the boundary, for example, between school and community; the boundary between teacher and student. Open education means that teachers can learn and that students can teach. It means a wide and open definition of educational resources. The power and the energy of open education come because educational resources are not confined to a single person in the classroom—the teacher—but are expanded and opened to include all members of the class or of the situation. This, of course, increases the unpredictability of the outcomes a thousandfold. To allow children to conduct independent investigations is already asking for trouble. You can be sure that they won't come up with the "right" answers. But to encourage them to work collaboratively, interdependently, is even more unsettling for the teacher, because it means that they may even discover that they don't need her.

Alternatively, the teacher may have to develop a new function, a new notion of academic or pedagogical leadership. Hence, open education is an important movement because it raises what is in a sense the central question of democracy. This is: How can we have both, on the one hand, wide participation and equality of human worth and, on the other hand, excellence of leadership? The answer to that question is to abandon the concept of the leader. The concept of the leader is essentially dichotomous for it implies another concept of the follower. We need to replace that dichotomous concept with a unitary concept of *leadership*. In a democracy, the functional concept of leadership implies that *all* may exercise leadership as appropriate. Leadership is a function that passes around as conditions change. Thus, the child develops self-management; that is, he leads himself when it is appropriate. He develops, moreover, the insights, the skills, the knowledge that enable him to exercise leadership when conditions indicate. This is the condition of interdependence and of what I understand as open education.

The circumstances were very favorable to open education after World War II. We had conditions of affluence, growth, confidence, high expectations. The stock market was rising to ever greater heights, and we knew with certainty that it would go on rising forever and ever, amen. Real wages were rising. It was similar to other conditions in history in other cultures when there has been a strong burgeoning of the human spirit and an opening up, a daring, a trying out of new ideas. I refer to periods like fifth-century Athens, like the Renaissance in Europe, like the industrial and agricultural revolutions in England.

Where are we now? Where have we come since 1968, which was a watershed? We're in a time of great challenge. Since 1968, the Nixon/Ford administrations have very skillfully engineered a situation that we have never had before, that is, a combination of high inflation and high unemployment with a fall in real wages. These are the ideal conditions for the exercise of maximum social control. When I say "maximum social control," I mean maximum predictability in social conditions, which is the opposite of open education. These are the conditions that create hierarchies, subordination, superordination, fear, concern for personal safety. The conditions are bad for open education. They're good for some other things, such as, campaigns against busing, campaigns of "back to the basics," campaigns for more discipline.

But there are many currents operating in the United States. One of the things that gives me most hope about the United States is that it's a country that seems to be able to allow a plurality of currents to coexist simultaneously. As people get a taste of the *Paree* of independence or interdependence, it's harder to keep them down on the farm of dependence.

Friedrich Froebel, who founded the first kindergarten in 1837 in Germany, was one of the first to appreciate the importance of the early years in development of the child and the role of play in that development. In his "garden of children" he encouraged children to explore, to express themselves, and to learn by doing and real-life experiences. Association for Childhood Education International.

Kindergarten in the North End Industrial Home, Boston, 1881, where Associated Charities taught the poor homemaking skills and provided them with job training and jobs, day care, education, inexpensive meals and entertainment. Library of Congress.

Early Progressive Schools—I

... that's about all we can ask for children—that they take an experience, fit it to some other that has gone before, develop new concepts, and then keep on building and building....

NEITH HEADLEY • Many people speak about the fact that they started teaching at a very early age. At least professionally, I can't say that. But I can say that I was interested from an early age in being a kindergarten teacher, and that's what I've been and enjoyed in my life. I've taught kindergarten children, and at the University of Minnesota I taught girls and boys who were going to be teachers in the early childhood field, and I've worked with parents. But I can't say that I began that very early. When I was young, it was not possible to get a college degree in the field of kindergarten education. You either had to go to a two-year teachers' college or to a teachers' training course, or something of that sort, and then, later, follow up your degree. I chose to do it the other way around. I went to Carleton College, knowing all the time that I wanted to be a kindergarten teacher, and took courses that I knew would be helpful later—courses in art, for instance, where I could get something that had a craft angle to it, and courses in music, and, particularly, courses in storytelling. I have always enjoyed children's books and children's stories and was able to do a good deal of undergraduate work in storytelling. When I completed my work at Carleton, I went on to Wheelock College and specialized in the kindergarten program. I did in one year the work that, elsewhere, I probably would have done in two years. From there, I went out into the field of actually being a teacher.

As an undergraduate, I had the opportunity—and I think it is an opportunity—to major in philosophy, and I have never regretted that. I certainly like the practical side of things—of biology and education and sociology and languages and zoology, and so forth, but I never regretted having the background in philosophy. I think back to how one delightful professor used to define philosophy, saying that philosophy is a science which treats of the wholeness of things. I think that that's a tremendous statement. I think perhaps that's been my outlook on early childhood education all along the way. It wasn't just that you learned this and then you checked it off, and learned something else and so forth, but that you fitted it together as you went along. I'm sure that's been one reason why it's not been such a shock to me to see the changes that are coming in education. I was quite convinced of the need for treating the wholeness of things when I was teaching at the University of Minnesota. Much as we would bend our every effort to help people build a philosophy of education in keeping with the best and in keeping with the times, we found that our students would go back to the way they were brought up. And that's exactly what I'm saying here. I had that opportunity—and I think I was lucky in having that opportunity—to live in an environment where I learned from experience. It seems to me that's about all we can ask for children—that they get experiences, and that they don't just get them in and check them off but that they take an experience, fit it to some other that has gone before, develop new concepts, and then keep on building and building, until the whole thing fits together in a philosophy which is a wholeness, which deals with a wholeness of things.

As far as actual teaching—I think we jumped from the facts that I was graduated from Carleton College, and then went to Wheelock College, and then did work at Harvard and, later, at Columbia. Aside from that, I had the experience of having my own private kindergarten for one year in my own college town, which was quite an experience; I wouldn't have missed it for anything, although it wasn't very practical. And then I had the opportunity to be in a public school kindergarten in

St. Paul. In those days—I think it was kind of ideal—we didn't go in as teachers who were supposed to be full-blown teachers, but as assistants. We were an assistant to a teacher who had had a great deal of experience. The only trouble with that situation for me was that the teacher was distressed about me for several reasons. One, I always wanted to sit on the tables, which I realized was not the right thing, but I liked it; and the other was that she used to look at me and my enthusiasm and say—she didn't say it in words but she used to look at me as if to say—"You'll get over it, you'll get over your enthusiasm, you'll run down." I don't really think I ever did. I think every challenge that was offered in the way of working with children or working with people has always been kind of thrilling. It distresses me to hear teachers who are "bored with it all." I can't see how anybody could be bored with it all, if one had an overall feeling of living and helping other people live more richly.

After St. Paul, my next experience was going back to Boston and teaching in a private school. I didn't want to, at all, and yet the opportunity was ripe, and I'm ever so glad that I did. I taught a kindergarten and a first grade combined, which is, again, very modern. It was delightful because we were in a big, lovely old home and it took a lot of courage to get a workbench moved into a mahogany-panelled living room, which was our classroom. But the person with whom I was working was enthusiastic about it.

It took a lot of determination, in a sense, to decide to go back to the University of Minnesota, which I never regretted, too. I've often wondered about the person who was head of the department at that time. Through the many years I was there, I never quite felt that he understood what it was all about. I remember his calling me into his office after I had been there only a few days—I had never met him myself, I had been hired by the person who was the head of the nursery school at Columbia. He put his feet up on the desk and looked over at me, saying, "Having a good time, having fun?" It distressed me no end, because I surely was having fun, and I thought the man much bigger than that. The next time I saw him, he came into the kindergarten room, looked around, and said, "Is Miss Headley here?" At that particular moment,

I was up on top of the jungle gym—I wanted to see if it would be dangerous for children, how much you could sway it—and he thought, again, I was having a right good time. And I *was* having a good time; I was having a great time. But I never did convince him, I think, that it wasn't *just* "having a good time," that you really should be doing something a little more worthwhile along the way. He was an interesting person; he did a great deal of writing. He's been quoted a great deal through the years, but he never quite understood what early childhood education was about. He thought that it was wasting a lot of the time when you worked entirely with young children. I wish he were alive still—so that he could see what we mean by the tremendous importance of the early years. It is not that academicians like him didn't think early childhood education was important, but that they thought it was important only from the point of view of pure research.

My thinking did not have to do with pure research. It had to do with living, and learning through living. I liked what a little girl said about her own philosophy—and perhaps I can conclude with it—when she and her mother spotted her kindergarten teacher in a grocery store, some years after her kindergarten experience. "Mother, I like her, she was a good teacher." On the way home, the girl's mother asked her if she knew why she liked the kindergarten teacher, and why she thought she was a good teacher. "Well, for one thing," the girl said, "she had lots of good ideas."

Early Progressive Schools—II

What the method is I can't tell you. The method was a matter of leading rather than telling. And constantly reverting to the children's enactment of their new knowledge. We would do this in dance, in music, in a dramatic play, whatever, so long as the children had an opportunity to give back the ideas that they were learning.

CHARLOTTE B. WINSOR • I'd like to reminisce a bit about John Dewey. When I was a very young and rebellious undergraduate at Teachers College and John Dewey was almost a guru to teachers of that day, I made my way in to his course. From our present outlook, we would say that he was most authoritarian. Seats were assigned by number, according to the alphabet. Since my name began with a *B*, I had to sit in a seat in the very first row. Then his assistants would walk up and down the aisle and take attendance which was compulsory. My problem was that he was so dull as a lecturer, and so dry, it was hard to keep awake. And there I was sitting right in front. It was really an ordeal.

The next time I met Dewey was a few years later, during my short foray into the labor movement. I was privileged—and it *was* a privilege—to go downtown to the shabby offices of the Clothing Cutters Union of the Amalgamated Clothing Workers of America. John Dewey looked 100 years old to me, but he was probably in his seventies by that time. He would come down every Sunday morning and talk to these people. He was such a different John Dewey on those mornings that I think it's worth telling about. At that time, he was *the* brightest professor of education in America. I don't know why I remember those mornings as so cold; perhaps it is because I felt sorry for this old man who had to come down there. But every Sunday morning he came to talk to those clothing cutters, most of them struggling with the English language, trying to get from him a sense of the philosophical meanings of the American scene.

My third episode with John Dewey was his 90th birthday party, which was held in one of those huge hotel rooms in Manhattan. What was interesting about it for me was how vividly it demonstrated his influence on the world. First, here was his life and work spread out before him, and there were the labor leaders of the country, the teachers, the professors. At the end of the evening, after many speeches had been made, the chairman got up and said, "We have an interesting bit of information. Nehru and his daughter, Indira, are in New York attending a UN Conference. They have heard about this dinner to honor John Dewey, and if you would like to wait, they would like to come and pay their respects." And they did come. It was a very moving tribute.

Now about schools, which is really my world. I could entertain you with accounts of the way the progressive experimental schools were perceived in the "olden days." A few *New Yorker* cartoons come to mind. One was a cartoon of a child looking up at a teacher, saying, "Do I have to do what I want to do *all* the time?" This was a favorite remark when anybody talked about these schools which many people saw as having no structure, no adult strictures, where the kids were running the show. Another cartoon showed a teacher wearing a dunce cap, sitting on the high chair in the classroom where the teacher used to sit when she wanted to be particularly authoritarian, and there were these little monsters running around the teacher. But my point is that I don't think these comments are just for fun. They also tell you something about how the early attempts to free the child were received by the lay world. More than that, there was tremendous distortion of the meaning of what these educators were trying to do. When anybody heard that you taught at City and Country School, for example, you were the butt of dinner table jokes and conversations, and almost all the time had to defend your position in the world. It was fun to do; I don't look back on it sadly. But there was a very serious, real meaning for all of this because I believe—and the talk this morning certainly backed me up—that education was a much larger concept than schools. Featherstone touched upon how Dewey and his followers thought that the schools could change the society, and some of my very recent colleagues still talk about schools as the major change agent on the American scene. The real issue, I think, is that the schools are a reflection of the society, and have to do a very slow, arduous, and thoughtful job to make an impression on children and their world.

To me, one of the most dramatic expressions of this is the effect on classrooms of Sputnik. I remember it as the time when the American society declined into a national inferiority complex. And bang, the schools were to blame! It has always angered me that the first really heavy federal money that came to the schools was under the aegis of the National Defense Education Act. I don't think other people minded it—they were so glad to have the money—but I minded it terribly that when people awoke to the fact that in education there was an important arm of cultural change it had to come under the aegis of fighting our adversaries, as our President said.

So the breadth of education means, as I see it, that at any instant it is a reflection of the social-cultural scene. To make that point further, I'd like to read to you from John Dewey, a piece that he wrote in 1952 when he was, I think, past 90. You may not place that date, but 1952 stands in my mind as the time of the McCarthy era, as a growing death. And it was people like John Dewey, incidentally, who were held to account by the McCarthyites for everything that was wrong in our society.

> During the past few years, organized attacks on the achievements of progressive education have become more extensive and virulent than ever before. The current effort to turn the clock back in education is real cause for alarm but not for surprise. The educational system is part of a common life and cannot escape suffering the consequences that flow from the conditions prevailing outside of the schools. The repressive and reactionary forces are in such entrenched strength in all our other institutions that it would be folly to expect the schools to get off free.

It would be folly to think that the progressive education movement was something thought up and put over by the teachers all by themselves. On the intellectual side, it was part of a wider movement of thought, the inquiry into the nature and problems of growth, which constitute the great contributions of the second half of the 19th century to the advancement of human knowledge in the biological, psychological, and sociological sciences. On the social side, it was part of a widespread effort to liberate individuals and institutions from bondage to repressive modes of life. Without the support of the progressive and enlightening forces in the community, both intellectual and social, the teachers of 'new vision' would have been at best ineffectual angels, born out of their time, and all their best plans and ideas would have had little or no effect on the educational system.

This was Dewey's attempt to defend what he thought of as the progressive movement in education. Progressive education is a term for which I would use a small *p*, because in my experience it has provided an umbrella for so many and such diverse ideas. The people responsible for the schools they founded, some of which I want to tell you about, would be uncomfortable if they were seen as a monolithic group. Enormous and continous controversy raged about this school or that school and whether each school was doing what was basic to its philosophy. But there are two very different strands of thinking associated with changing the schools, one, a progressive style in schooling and the other, an experimental style, both of which were emerging at this time in this country. In the minds of the people who founded these schools, and especially in the minds of the experimentalists, the progressive schools were concerned with pedagogic improvement through which children's development would be attained. In other words, they were concerned with teaching the kids more efficiently, with broader educational goals. That is no small improvement in education.

At that time, many universities, through their departments of education, ran laboratory schools. The Lincoln and Horace Mann Schools were two of the schools I knew here in New York City that were carrying on this kind of 'progressive movement' in their way of teaching and in curriculum development. Another was the Dalton School. The Dalton Plan offered (and still offers) the child a contract to fulfill. At the old Lincoln School, a tremendous amount of experimental work was done on the development of workbooks. Some of you who have been teaching since then know the powerful influence of workbooks in schools. (I remember, many years later, talking to a young man who was working very hard on teaching machines. When I said, "You know, in a way, it seems to me that the teaching machine is an electronic workbook," he said with surprise, "You're right, that's just what it is.") Well, in each case the educators in the early period of progressive education were telling us, in very familiar words, that what they were hoping for was the child's independence, that he would use these workbooks on his own initiative. But basically they were preparing the child for the status quo.

Now I wish to turn to the experimental group, responsible for founding a number of schools, each implementing a broadly-based philosophy of education. The first is the City and County School, which I know very well indeed because I was teaching there in the days when many of these ideas were being developed and carried out. Another is the Walden School, with which I've had a good deal of connection through my students. A third is the Little Red Schoolhouse, which many know or have heard about. And the fourth is the Nursery School which was started as part of the Bank Street College. When these schools were started, their founders were told, "You had better document what you are trying to do so that someone will know what it is all about." Let me offer Carolyn Pratt's first attempt to explain why she was starting the City and Country School:

> We aim to attempt the revision of school practice, *from the ground up*, by discarding at the beginning of our work all the traditional preconceptions that govern the standard practice of the schools today. In the course of our school's development, provisions in regard to programs, curriculum, and method have been adopted *only* as they have appeared to be justified by the *school's own experiences* and the situations which arise in our classrooms.

In this same account, Miss Pratt goes on to say:

What the organism needs is opportunity, and the business of pedagogy is to provide opportunity while the organism can establish itself. This opportunity lies in the environments of the children wherever they happen to be, it cannot be elsewhere. The assumption of the schools that children can only understand their own environment by approaching it from environments far apart from their own experience is putting all the carts in the world before all the horses and, furthermore, confusing the horse and cart relationship beyond redemption.

This second quote is from the introduction Carolyn Pratt wrote to one of the first publications to come out of City and Country School, which was called, interestingly enough, *Before Books*. It was an extensive record of a classroom for four-year-olds and six-year-olds that Miss Jessie Stanton had taught. What is interesting about that introduction is its title, "Pedagogy as a Creative Art," and that most of it deals with the experience of the artist and how he experiences life. Miss Pratt talks about the teaching-learning equation, which is really learning as an inner-directed activity and, therefore, an artistic experience for both the teacher and the child. A cardinal principle of these educators was that learning is an inner-directed experience, an entirely different process from one in which the teacher gives and the child takes. We see the child as an operating being, rather than as a vessel into which the adult pours experience. That was, and is, a truly radical concept. The process through which this happens is play structured by the adult, but offering the child true autonomy of expression. In fact, the first name of the City and Country School was the Play School.

Another experimental school, the Walden School, developed its philosophy and program on the basic premises of psychoanalysis. It was founded by Margaret Naumburg, who later became a rather well-known child analyst. She called her approach the *one direct method* of education. And she says in this early bulletin describing the school:

Up to the present, our methods of education have dealt only with the conscious or surface mental life of the child. The new analytic psychology has, however, demonstrated that the unconscious mental life of the child, which is the outgrowth of the child's instincts, plays a greater role as a conscience. The new psychology has uncovered the true nature of permanent thought and has shown that it still lives on in the unconscious mental being of the adult, as well as of the child. Up to the present time, education has missed the real significance of the child's behavior. . . . In fact, the medium of speech, even when it is mastered as a channel of inquiry and articulation, is often blocked by the false answers of grownups to the child's earliest questionings as to life, birth, and death. In consequence, the child is forced back to the expressions of each problem in the more primitive language of symbolic form—in his drawings, his dancing, his music, and his other activities.

I am interested in this statement, written in 1918, because in recent years, with the concern about cognitive development, there has been such emphasis on language development. I offer this not necessarily because I agree with it, but because I think that it is important that we respect the intellectual stance and understand the social scene in which those people lived and worked.

Another school that was designed by members of this group of radical pioneers was the Little Red Schoolhouse. It was originally an experiment in the public school system in the teens of the century, when the New York City Board of Education gave Elisabeth Irwin a shabby little building. What Elisabeth Irwin was trying to do was to offer a good school experience for all children. They were going to work in one classroom on each grade. They carried that experiment for some time, using volunteers (among them, Lucy Sprague Mitchell) to work with the teachers and children. What I think undid them was their success. The parents of the Greenwich Village community were a sophisticated group who understood what was a good school for their children. When they heard about these experimental classes, they began to put pressure on the school to have their children given places there and that got to be a bit embarrassing for the rest of the teachers and the rest of the school. So on the basis of the proposition that there was no money for this experiment, although, as far as I know, they didn't put any money into it, the board gave up the experiment in 1931. Consequently, in one hot summer, the parents who had their children in those classes got together, bought an old parish house in Bleecker Street, painted it red, refurbished it, got some secondhand furniture, and opened the Little Red Schoolhouse as a private institution.

What they wanted to demonstrate was that they could provide what one might call a good, or modern, or progressive school life for children under conditions that were very similar to the conditions of a number of the experimental and progressive schools that were functioning in the city at that time. There was a tuition charge. In 1931, the per capita cost in New York City public schools was $160 for a year! So their tuition was put at $160 when they started. For the older children, they were going to have classes of the size that the city schools had, classes between 35 and 40 children. They were going to (and still do) make very concentrated use of student teachers who came from nearby Bank Street, New York University, and other teacher education programs. They admitted children on the basis that the public schools admitted their children—no tests, no interviews, no fancy psychological finding-out when you weaned your child and how it reacted and all that sort of thing. All of this was a very popular procedure in those days. But they were accepting children from all over the city, from any parents willing to send them.

Agnes de Lima, who wrote the book, *The Little Red Schoolhouse*, said that they could and would benefit from the mistakes of the other progressive schools because they started their school as a private institution some 12 years later than the others. And maybe they did. I will say that their goals, their social commitments, have been manifested in their curriculum development throughout the years. In the nursery and primary years—they started at age four—the program was very similar to that of the City and Country School, or what later became the Bank Street College Nursery School, or the Walden School. But in the upper years, beginning at about age eight, all of these schools put a great deal of stress on the development of social studies curriculum. And in this school—now I am recalling my own experience—there was a definite recognition that people in various parts of the world had rebelled from repression and that these were the people they wanted their children to know about. Many years ago, just after a revolution in Mexico, the fourth grade studied Mexico before and after the Revolution. In later years, they studied the story of the Jewish people and the black people long before this became a concern of curriculum generally. They studied the history of the USSR, of China.

I'm not saying that some of this content did not exist in some of these other schools. But I'm saying that at Little Red they focused on it. The head of that school for many years was Randolph Smith and I remember his announcing that they took it upon themselves to have their children become aware of how the peoples of the world reacted to repressive conditions. Don't get an idea that in these schools they waited until the children found out everything. There would be a great deal of teacher input, and a heavy reliance on books. They rarely worked as a class of 40. They would come together as a class for some general discussions, for the presentation of material. But there would be a great deal of work in small groups with student teachers working with the children, and most important, an emphasis on knowledge of people, their way of life, their art, their music, their customs, their myths, their religion. The methodology was research, reading, recording, dramatizing, doing. And I should say that such an approach was common to all these schools that I have mentioned.

Then there was another school that I was with—actually a research institution. That was the school that later became the Bank Street School for Children. It started basically to pass on the research work of the Bureau of Educational Experiments, which was the foundation upon which Bank Street was built. They felt they needed children because they were going to do research about children. And the first group that they developed independently was the nursery school, which Harriet Johnson headed. She was a trained nurse, by the way. It was a very small group with a very large staff, and they compiled many records because they were masters of recording. In her first days, Miss Johnson was asked, "Why do you want a school for children under three?" And she said, "Our first answer is in terms of educational needs. We feel that the educational factors of the environment for babies"—and this really rings a very modern bell when we're talking about infant programs—"the educational factors in the environment for babies need study and planning as much as, and perhaps more than, those in the environment of older children." Her second answer was in terms of research:

> We feel the need of 'scientific' data concerning children and growth—and growth of every sort that is measurable or observable. Now, what can we say about the educational needs for babies under three? We try to design an environment which is designed for babies, designed to give them rich sensory and motor experiences, designed to give them appropriate learning through experimentation, designed to give them adventure without danger to life or limb, designed to give them contact with their peers without demanding inappropriate adjustment. In short, an environment planned with educational needs in mind.

John Dewey—in that same article in which he was defending progressive education from the onslaught of the McCarthyism of the 1950s—ends with what I think is basic to practice in schools, whether they be open education or experimental schools or progressive education:

> For the creation of a democratic society, we need an educational system where the process of moral and intellectual development is in practice, as well as in theory, a cooperative transaction of inquiry engaged in by free independent human beings who treat ideas and the heritage of the past as means and effort for further enrichment of life, both quantitatively and qualitatively, and who use the good obtained for the establishment of something better.

I would love it if you would talk critically about what went on in the classrooms that was very different from what was going on in the public schools.

Well, when I was teaching, I would get this group of children, 22 in number. I would know the teacher who had them the year before. We were required to write very full records at the end of the year, so I knew a lot about these children. I knew them in the halls; it was a small school. But one of the things I would make myself do, first of all, is take a look at their academic standing. And I can tell you that the range was very wide. I would have the fifth grade, and most of them were fairly good readers, but not up to fifth grade, not all of them. I would first take a very careful look at that. And then I would put it in the back of my mind. I was the classroom teacher—you could call it a contained classroom—but I had a music teacher working with me, as well as a dance teacher, a shop teacher, a science teacher, and a marvelous children's library run by Margaret Ernst, an authority on language, and not only children's language. I had all these resources. I really want to make it very clear that, while some of us get this kind of nostalgic euphoria about how wonderful we were—and I think we tried to be wonderful—we had an awful lot going for us anyway. But my first thought was to develop my program. And after that we would have three days of teachers' meetings before school started. So that you had to have some thoughts on the subject. You had to say something about what you were planning for the kids, because we had no textbooks, we had no curriculum that was given.

Before I go on, I should explain that at City and Country, they had, and still have, what is called a "job program." At the third-grade level, at eight, the children run the school post office, which includes doing a serious job of maintaining all the communications within the school. Out of that they study communications. In other words, social studies arises from the job that the children do for their school. Now, this is a thought that is difficult to carry through, but I wish more schools would do it. Because when they are moving into these years, it gives the children a wonderful sense of competence. It gives them responsibility. And it gives them a sense of importance about their role in the society of the school.

Now, if a 10-year-old whom I was teaching had a job to do—say the hand printing for the school, making the signs and posters and so on—it was my job to build on it, at least in my thinking. What do you have to learn if you're learning about printing? And how do people communicate to begin with? I remember doing dramatizations of smoke signals and drum signals and ultimately, we began to study these and other forms of symbolic communication, which takes you back to some of the earliest cultures.

My point is that as we were developing our skills we were also talking about the fact that people learn how to talk to each other in many ways. And my curriculum that year developed out of that. I taught it for several years, but in very different ways, depending on what went on between the children. And then we began to study the people around the eastern end of the Mediterranean Sea: the Phoenicians, the Hebrews, the Egyptians, the Greeks, and the Romans to find out what the lives of these people were like, what they wore, what they grew, and so forth. I'm simply saying that this is how we began. What the method is I can't tell you. The method was a matter of leading rather than telling. And constantly reverting to the children's enactment of their new knowledge. We would do this in dance, in music, in a dramatic play, whatever, so long as the children had an opportunity to give back the ideas that they were learning.

How did I structure space? At the City and Country School, and this is true in these other schools that I've been talking about, in the early years, the space was kept very open. In the City and Country School, for very specific reasons, the major chunk of space was for blockbuilding. As I look back, my experience with these children up to the age of six and seven—the amount of creative life that they were able to express in their blockbuilding—was almost reverent. Maybe reverent is too strong a word. That makes it seem as if I can't remember all the hard times I had getting them to pick up the blocks. But what I mean by that is the independence, the autonomy, that children could express in their blockbuilding was fantastic.

So we did have space in what I would call the pre-academic years. The space was very open and very malleable. I never got used to the idea that you had this area or that area or the other area because in my classroom, you know, it was convenient to have the two easels and the paints near the sink, so that's where it was. But there were times when nobody seemed to be using the easels so I would fold them up, put them away, or put them against the wall or something. The areas were not set. I didn't need a science area. We had a science room where we could go and get the material, but we did a lot of science experiments in connection with our blockbuilding. I remember we had batteries because we wanted to light our building. I remember one group got me almost crazy because they wanted to develop a reservoir! In the upper grades, there was a classroom, not a very big room, there were tables and there were chairs, and I remember how shocked those teachers were when I said, "You know, I taught children for 20 years and I never had a desk." How could you be a teacher—what would you sit behind—if you didn't have a desk! Anyway, there were tables and chairs and, incidentally, depending on the teacher, it made very little difference to me whether those tables were in rows or around in a circle or anything else. There were times when I wanted the kids to talk, to talk with me, and we'd bring our chairs up some place where we could talk together. And sometimes I wanted each one to sit at his desk, when there was arithmetic or spelling, and the tables and chairs were arranged that way. But in the rooms themselves there wasn't need for so much of this extra material because we had specialist classrooms. On the other hand, when it came time for doing a play, the tables and chairs were very often stacked in the back of the room days on end while we were painting the scenery or rehearsing the play or sewing our costumes or doing all of the things that you needed to do. So the one word that I could answer that question on space with is, perhaps, *flexibility*.

During the Depression, F.E.R.A. (Federal Emergency Relief Administration) provided jobs for unemployed teachers and care for the neediest children by funding nurseries such as the one above (in Illinois). Association for Childhood Education International.

Early Progressive Schools—II

Federal funding of nurseries continued through World War II, when many mothers joined the production lines. The nursery above was in New York City. Schomburg Library.

The First Day Care Program

Whether you know it or not, whether you are aware of it or not, the past is with you and has to be. If you can pick it up and carry it and get the benefits of it, take its treasure and leave the dross, you keep on.

CORNELIA GOLDSMITH • I was five years old in 1897 and kindergartens were where the nursery school is today. Kindergartens had not yet moved into the public schools, but they were available on a private basis. I went to a kindergarten, which was then a Froebelian kindergarten. Friedrich Froebel of Germany had exported the idea that children, particularly young children—and this was a very novel thought—could learn through play. This is why he called it "the garden of children," the *kinder garten*; it was a garden of play. Children could learn and be in a happy environment and be accepted and have their set games called "gifts and occupations" and learn about the weather, and the thermometer, and the day of the week, and hot and cold, and near and far—all these things could be learned through play and games. So I went to a private kindergarten at the age of five and had a very happy time. We played circle games, we learned finger play, and we sang: "Here's a ball for baby, big and soft and round. Here's the baby's hammer, oh, how he can pound." It stayed with me. "Here's the big umbrella to keep the baby dry, here's the baby's cradle, rockabye baby bye." The things that we remember our whole lives long that have had sparkle very often have been first experiences.

But let me tell you, at the end of that year—very pleasant, very friendly—I entered the public school. And that memory is

The First Day Care Program

so clear, I can give you every detail of it. It has lived for 80 some years, and vividly lived. I stepped into a classroom, rows of seats fastened to the floor, each desk with a little pen place and a little ink place, each desk with a little book place and Miss Madigan was the teacher. Her hair was down close, parted in the middle. She was rather plump. She had a friendly face, and she was what was called "firm." I was in row two. "Will row one please stand," Miss Madigan would say. Well, first you would have to put your feet flat on the floor and fold your hands and listen. "Row one please stand, turn, march to the blackboard." The room had blackboard surface around the entire room. At each place, there was an eraser and a piece of chalk. We stood with our backs to the blackboard waiting for the next instruction and Miss Madigan would say, "Pick up your chalk, leave the eraser alone, and write your initials." I must have come from a very backward home. First time she said that I didn't know what an initial was. But I knew I wasn't supposed to copy because you cheat when you learn from somebody else. So I looked surreptitiously to the child on my right, and I looked surreptitiously to the child on my left, and they didn't seem at all alike, even though the order had been one and the same. So I carefully took a little from here, and took a little from there, and marked it on the blackboard. Miss Madigan began walking around the room scrutinizing our initials. I wasn't sure what would happen. It might have been a bomb or an explosion. Instead she patted me on the head and said, "Very nice, Cornelia." I was very pleased that I had been so successful. When I went home, I asked my mother, "What in the world is an initial?" When she explained and said, "How could you combine other people's initials and do 'very nice work'?"—I learned to mistrust educators from then on. They didn't always mean what they said.

And so it went through the public school, with little variety. It just was like that and one accepted it. But then came a time of getting further training. I finished high school and I knew what I wanted to do. My friends were in conflict about what direction to go in, but I think because of my position in my own family, I was clear. I was the oldest girl in a family of five, with three younger sisters whom I loved dearly and with whom I worked to the point where they called me their second mother. I could get them to make beds with me any time by telling them a story. I learned my storytelling from bedmaking. I knew I wanted to work with children, and they had to be young children. I really wanted to work with children at the beginning of their social lives, the beginning of their learning of speech, the beginning of their interacting. There were no nursery schools, they hadn't been heard of. So kindergarten was the closest I could come to what I wanted and I found a place in the local teacher training institution, where you could be prepared to teach all grades if you just got your certificate. The only trouble was that there was no course in kindergarten. I was a very shy, reticent young woman, but I got up the courage to go to the principal, whose name I still remember even though I remember current friends' names very little. "Mr. Eberly," I said, "I'm interested in kindergarten education." And he said, "We don't offer it yet." And I said, "But I still want it." And he said, "There's only one way that you can get it and that is to persuade your friends to come in as a class and we'll give you a class in kindergarten education." I don't remember how I did this, but I persuaded a classful, and in they came, and we had a class in kindergarten education. After two years, I graduated with a kindergarten diploma and an elementary school certificate.

When I graduated I felt very educated indeed. I knew how to write a lesson plan. I knew all about the Froebelian method, having practiced it, as well as having learned how to teach it. And I began professional life as an assistant kindergartener in the demonstration kindergarten connected with the training school. (Even though it didn't teach the subject, the school had a demonstration kindergarten.) From there, after a year and a half of work as an assistant kindergarten teacher, I went into a public school in St. Paul, Minnesota, at a salary which seemed munificent at the time—$60 a month. I was living at home, of course, and it was just gorgeous to have $60 a month. But after a short while—to help take care of a set of aging grandparents—I went to California, and there my certificate in elementary education was very convenient.

I began teaching in a crowded public school, whose children were drawn from the waterfront district and from a half dozen different backgrounds. And the curriculum that I was expected to enforce wasn't suitable. I just could do nothing with it. So, again, I got up my courage, because I was very idealistic—I wanted to educate in the very best way—and went to the superintendent and said to him, "This curriculum doesn't let me educate." He said to me, "You're a very well-trained teacher. What is it you want?" I said, "I want more freedom. I want more leeway. I want more flexibility." He said, "Well, let's make a compromise. Have your freedom and your flexibility, but at the end of the year those children have to meet the standards." I said, "That's fine, as long as I can be flexible in the meantime, they'll probably go beyond the standards."

I had a gorgeous time, but actually I cheated. We had all of these special teachers, who came to teach the children how to produce art, how to sing, how to do all the specialties. The children were supposed to be very sympathetic to these people. But to my way of thinking, they were all very strange to the children and they didn't really belong. We could have done what they did and done it better. At least that's how we felt in our conceit. So I said to the children, "I am now going to go out of the room and I am going to come back as Miss so-and-so, the music teacher." It turned into a game. I came in and said, "Feet flat on the floor"—and they all went down with a plump. "Hands folded, sit up straight, draw a deep breath, and say ah"—and they did it. I said, "Now I'm going to teach you a little song." They got into the spirit of this so beautifully that when the music teacher came in, they were all rehearsed. They were an ideal group, just perfect.

But then there came an opening in a kindergarten, which was always my first love. This was my first directorship of a kindergarten. I found myself in a beautiful kindergarten building, with a playground around it, with lots of space, with plenty of equipment, and with three assistants. The only drawback here was that I was presented with 75 children aged five, and it was impossible. I said to myself, "With your slow mind, it'll take you at least a semester to learn all their names and then it'll take the next semester to see them out into the next step." So, again, I gathered my courage, went to the principal, and said, "Mrs. Aufkauf, I can't teach 75 children. All I can do is police them and keep them out of mischief and out of trouble." She said, "Well, what's your solution?" I said I didn't know. So she said, "go to the superintendent, perhaps he can help you." So I went through the same rigamarole with the superintendent. His question was, "Well, what's your solution?" But I suddenly had a bright idea. I said, "Why couldn't I take the older half of the children in the afternoon and the younger half of the children in the morning so they can go home and have their naps in the afternoon. I'll divide the assistants; I'll keep one assistant in the morning and two in the afternoon, and it will be ideal." He said, "You know your contract; you'll get no more money." I wasn't worried about the money. I was living at home, my expenses were paid, and the money was inconsequential. So we started the two-session kindergartens in southern California.

But I had a conflict—and this conflict stayed with me for many, many years. When I went into the public schools, they were rigid. Absolutely inflexible. They had their curriculum, and you were a disciplinarian first and an educator second, if there was time left over. So I tried the private schools. The private schools had plenty of flexibility. The trouble was they were over-flexible; anything went. Children were brought from wealthy homes in chauffeur-driven cars and catered to and catered to and catered to. The children had become sort of blasé. They expected everything to be done for them. And this kind of school was intolerable to me, too. So I moved back and forth, back and forth, from public to private, from public to private seeking some situation where one could have the benefits of the private and the benefits of the public, where all children would be welcome, where they wouldn't be divided according to levels of financing in the family. Suddenly one morning, after 10 years in southern California, which was really beautiful, I said to myself, "You never really finished your education in that two-year teacher training school. Why don't you get educated?"

At that time, the source of all education in the field of early childhood was at Teachers College, Columbia University. So I hied me out there. I had to work my way through,

The First Day Care Program 153

but I hit the university at the time when Dewey and Kilpatrick were teaching. I took a placement in one of the experimental progressive schools, where, suddenly, I found everything I had been looking for—the Walden School when Margaret Naumburg was the director. I also found myself in a very peculiar situation. Teachers College was curious about this whole progressive education idea and had me make reports to them about what was happening at the Walden School. I felt that I was being used, if not abused. So I finally broke away from Teachers College and went fulltime into the Walden School.

The Walden School was a sparkle in my life from beginning to end, full of challenge, full of difficulty, full of all sorts of new ideas. And with the teaching going on at the college at the same time, it was a stimulus of the first order. But then I married, and with the marriage came a trip to England. We settled in Cambridge and I went into the business of making babies. I produced two female children, very sparkly. When I came back, I had enough feeling of security, perhaps, independence, perhaps, I don't know what, to set up my own nursery school for two-year olds. And that was one of the most adventurous, wonderful experiences that I ever had. These were children of professional people. There was much outcry at the time against taking children away from their family and their home; they belonged in the home, and didn't belong in a group. But it turned out well; there were many rich experiences, and at the request of the parents I moved those children, including my own two young ones, to the country for a summer. That was the beginning of a camp for young children that I ran for 15 years. The experience of actually living with a large group of children over 24 hours was a rare and wonderful one.

We made a film of that camp, which is called "A Child Went Forth." It happened very accidentally and by accident it has turned out to have lasting value. It was taken back in World War II, way back then. One day the father of my youngest camper, a moviemaker named Joseph Losey, came to me a week after camp began—his son was running barefooted on the ground—and said, "I have never seen such photogenic children in my life." I said, "All children are photogenic, if they are allowed to be natural, be themselves, have things to do and be content and happy." He said he would like to make a chronicle of his child's first experience away from home. Would I allow him to do it? I said, "I'd love to have a movie taken, but I have no money to pay you. There's nothing in the budget for this and I still have very high standards and regulations. Even if you paid for it, you'd have to meet my regulations." Joe asked what they were and I said, "For one thing, never pose a child. For another thing, take your chances with what you see; have a fearless operator who will see children who smite one another and then show what happens when they smite, who will see children in the nude, whether they're male or female, who will see children as they are." I went on telling him exactly what I wanted until he said, "How would it be if I took the picture, you minded your business, I minded mine, and at the end we would only produce what you approved of?" I couldn't find fault with that; it met my obligations, and I agreed. He moved up for the summer, with a photographer, brought all his paraphernalia, his cameras, his mirrors, his hocus-pocus, and set them up day after day, letting the children gather around, flipping the cameras, turning the mirrors, changing all sorts of things, until they had finished with their questioning and their experimentations. Then the children went about their business and Joe went about his. There was no posing in the picture, which is one of its great assets. The other is that Joe spent the whole summer there. And although his son opens the picture stepping high through a field of daisies, he got so intrigued with the other children that it wasn't just a chronicle of his child, it was a chronicle of many of the children who attended the camp. I have only one regret about that picture and that is that it was made the year before I decided that this camp had to be truly interracial.

After that excursion, I went back to Walden with my little school and incorporated it into the larger school. They were then ready to take twos and push on further into this whole field of early childhood education; they made me director of their Lower School. Then one morning I awoke with a new conviction, that I needed to broaden my experience. I had been at Walden for a very long time and Walden was doing

The First Day Care Program

fine, but I felt I had better get out and I had better choose my next boss myself. The time comes, I think, when there's nothing more important than selecting your own boss. I selected Mary Shattuck Fisher Langer, who was then director of the nursery school program in early childhood at Vassar College, and I was plumped into a beautiful situation in a college teaching teachers and directing a group of children. I could give you many experiences there that were gleaming glitter. But instead, I'll skip ahead a lot of years to the war. In 1943 came a request that I move to New York City and direct a program that was then being set up by the New York City Department of Health to insure that children in day care agencies were given the protection and services guaranteed them under the law. The law had been on the books for awhile, but it had been disregarded and now it had been rewritten to establish some standards for service to the young children in group care. I had just signed my second three-year contract at Vassar, but my director said, "It is wartime. If you're needed there more than you're needed here, go, go, go. We will give you a year's leave of absence and if need be, we'll extend it a second year." As a matter of fact, I stayed for 20. And never got through. What caught up with me then was compulsory retirement. I lingered a little, but at 72 I was out, and with great reluctance.

What made the work so interesting was that there was no precedent for the program. It meant laying new foundation stones, initiating and starting again at the beginning of something that was of major importance. It meant a woman, an educator, being put in the position of directing a program that included all the professions that were involved in the field of early childhood: the pediatricians, the public health nurses, the social workers, the nutritionists next door, the sanitary engineers on the other side. It meant working in a governmental and administrative situation that was totally foreign to me. It meant pooling these efforts, and moving out into a city where nobody knew how many nurseries there were, how many preschool groups, how many children in preschool living. It meant making a first survey. It meant having the backing of a very high level, very well-informed advisory committee, which was helpful through many, many years.

And it meant pioneering. I discovered then that this entire field of early childhood has been a pioneering one since the beginning. It has pioneered and pioneered and pioneered and moved. With each step, it has moved ahead. And here was a new step, a governmental step.

With our first survey, we found that there were some 500 nursery groups where there were more than six children under six, all of which needed to be licensed, and that only about half of them came up to the standards that had been very carefully and very wisely set up. We were then faced with a big question. We had legal power to close any nursery that didn't meet the standards. Did we want to close that many? Did we want to throw these children back on the streets? Remember, it was still wartime. Many of these children were latch-key children, whose fathers were overseas, and whose mothers were busy. For the most part, they were left to their own devices and many exploiters had begun their exploitations. So it was a question of whether we wanted these children to go back to where they had come from or whether we were going to protect them. By good fortune, a decision was made that the nursery groups would be allowed time to come up to standards, indefinite time, if they showed sincerity and genuine effort in that direction.

We found conditions that you wouldn't believe possible. Incredible situations of exploitation of children. On the other hand, we were able to say, as we did to the nuns who ran nursery groups but who had had no education and who were working with young children with the best intentions in the world, "Find a way to improve your background, to get some learning in this field." At first, they couldn't find a way. No university had a department of early childhood education at the time. But finally Fordham opened one and the nuns could present plans for completing their training within five, 10, 15, 20 years. As long as they were moving, it was acceptable. Many people resisted the training and went in only because it was required, but when they came back afterwards, they had been convinced. "We didn't know," many said, "that there were all these books, all these people, all these situations in this field in which we're functioning. It has opened our eyes, our hearts, and our minds, and we are grateful."

The First Day Care Program

There was great activity at that time on the part of the colleges to set up departments for early childhood. Many of them set them up in such a way that the people who were already working in the field could take their courses on weekends and evenings. It stimulated a great deal of activity until finally, before I left, there were more than 1,000 so-called fully qualified teachers who were working within the 500 schools. We closed those schools that could not accept help, could not move, or were definitely exploiting children in incredible ways. These we took to court to close and won in every action. In fact, over and over, when these matters came up for trial, the judges would say, "You people have waited far too long." But we decided it was better to wait and be sure and have our evidence and not lose a case. We felt if we ever lost a case in court we would probably go down the drain altogether. Then the exploiters would move back in. People used to come from other parts of the country to ask for an appointment and say, "We hear there's money to be made here in child care. Would you tell us about the wealthiest neighborhoods that need good nurseries like ours?" We'd say, in effect, "There's no money to be made off kids. You can't make it because we're on the watchdog path and we would be watching you. You can be stopped." And they'd go to some other town and ask the same question. What happened there I don't know.

But the very interesting thing was that this small staff, composed of one social worker, one public health nurse, one halftime pediatrician, and one educator, developed into a staff of some 25 and we never had enough people. We had to make maximum use of every person. What we would have liked to do was to have teams of people go out to each center and be available where needed. But we had to make use of each individual. We had to select the individual who was to become the consultant to a given center in terms of the needs of that center. If the needs were largely physical, the pediatrician would go; if the needs were largely social, the social worker might go; or the educator might go. And each individual became the person responsible for helping that agency in whatever direction it most needed and wanted to go.

Everyone had freedom of access to people in other professions within the staff. They could call on someone to go with them and help them over some hurdle that the nursery group was meeting. And by this means, the pediatricians and the nurses and the educators learned the same language. You wouldn't believe it, but they learned to communicate. They learned to talk to each other. They had come in with very special languages, almost as if they had come from separate stars and didn't understand each other. It was a way of maintaining your independent importance. But by sharing, they learned a great deal. They also learned respect for each other's professions.

It was my long-held hope that ultimately a group of universities or colleges would get together—one that had an outstanding pediatric training program, one that had an outstanding social work program, one that had an outstanding early childhood program—with the idea of practicing together, deciding how they would share the responsibility of the welfare of these children. It seemed to me—and this began to happen when I got involved in Head Start—that we needed to find not just a means of cooperating, but a real working together by the professions. There was a great deal of jealousy between social workers and educators, pushing each other around a little to prove that one was more important than the other. It seemed important to me to get them to see eye-to-eye in terms of focusing on children. I remember at one point going up to Teachers College, my alma mater, and talking with Millie Almy about universities cooperating. She said, "You know, you're coming up against a few difficulties here. The universities are also competitive, and they're going to want to know who grants the diploma, who gathers the money, who will have more pupils. At this juncture, you're not going to be very successful." She was right. A great deal more effort needed to be expended before it could happen and I just walked out, because of old age.

But then, after sitting on my rump for a year, retired, trying to write a book, I had a request to take another job that was just as compelling and just as exciting and just as interesting as any I'd ever had and one I never dreamt would come my way. The job was executive director of the National Association for the Education of Young Children. So I said,

I'd do it by the fall. By then I'd be through with my book. But once my whole libido went in two directions, I found I couldn't write the book. I said goodbye to it for awhile, and went into an organization of national scope with a membership of 1,850 people. I stayed for a year and a half.

In that year and a half, the NAEYC grew from a membership of 1,850 to 14,000, and I was not equipped with staff or anything else to cope with it. It was a tumultuous time. I closed the little office in Chicago, opened a little office in New York, brought the two offices together, and then moved them both down to Washington where they really belonged. There Head Start was booming, interest in young children was booming. Everybody wanted to join; everybody wanted to become a part of this thing. And it just boomeranged. It just spread so fast, so rapidly, that I had to again pick up my little papers and walk out, just like that. With no notice, out I went. I always had the little book to come back to. And even after I finished it, after almost 10 years, as you will notice if you read it, I could not end it. Everything was openended at the time. All the unrest, all the new social situations were compelling, and I could not see the answer. I just could not. So finally I said, "Well, who has to end a book. What you do is just close it, just finish, stop writing." So it goes along and then, when it comes to telling you what the future should be and how we should all be moving toward open education, I just closed it. It's a book without an end for all of you to finish.

Early childhood education is still, I think, *the* field, because it's in the beginning that things matter, and these are the beginning years. And I think they are the most consequential and the most exciting and the most needing arm. There's so much to learn.

I think the essential lesson I learned about working with parents is that if there are basic differences between us, differences that need to be resolved, we need to expose them so that we can understand each other. When you talk about parent education, such as we have for a long time, parent education means our education, too. It's mutual education. I think acknowledging this basis of working with children means tremendous growth in human understanding. The parent is, after all, an educator, whether she knows it or not, likes it or not, knows she's doing it or not; she is an educator. She is a lifetime educator. She is setting the tone as long as the child is dependent. The teacher is supplementary in a sense. But the better a teacher can accept the parent, the better the mutuality of the experience. It seems to me that that is the essential aspect. Even in Head Start, where we had parent participants and volunteers, when I talked to the teacher I would say, "Why do you have only one parent functioning?" She'd say, "Well, the parents are a pain in the neck. They're so critical of us. I can teach better without the feeling of that criticism." This feeling—that teachers always know best and that they have had to educate the parent—has been built up over the years. The reverse has very seldom been seen as true. I think we have to bring it, as I say, beyond partnership, beyond cooperation, into the merging of the professions, the merging of whoever it is, teacher-educator, educator-parent.

What's my reaction to the move to make the public schools the prime sponsors of preschool education? Well, ultimately, I feel the young child needs to and will move into public school life. Unfortunately, as the kindergartens have moved into the system, they've been more systematized and not been in a position to affect the system. But I don't agree with those who have said that the system is still rigid and can't be penetrated, that it has a stone wall around it and has built its own future. My feelings have been that within the system there are always people who will help chip from the inside out, as well as people who will chip from the outside in to help liberalize the system. I think we're seeing some loosening up. Much too slow, and it takes too long. But it is happening. And it will happen, I think, more and more. I think if teachers who are in the public school system move towards freer ways of expression, there's a contagion in this because they are happier people and they are easier people to live with and to work with. And they mean more to children.

I'd like to close on this note. Whether you know it or not, whether you are aware of it or not, the past is with you and has to be. If you can pick it up and carry it and get the benefits of it, take its treasure and leave the dross, you keep on.

Residential Programs

... Not to change the differences ... I think the differences are valuable ... but to learn to live with each other and to learn something about each other's culture. Not to use differences as a barrier, but to use them as a bridge.

WALTER E. CLARK ● At the age of five, I started as a pupil in a one-room country school, spartan and strict. You've read about them: The long desks and the benches, the potbellied wood-burning stove in the center, the well and the pump outside, the flagpole, and, of course, the two outhouses with a long, high fence separating them. A large open play area on a hillside, a stream, a farm next door with fruit trees, grapes, and berries, which we raided with great pleasure. The open part of those schools was the recess, and walking back and forth to school. That was the time for talking and laughing and playing and chasing and for social exchange. Totally unstructured, totally child-initiated in every way, those schools were small and essentially very friendly. You knew everyone in the school before you ever went there because all of them were your neighbors, and many of them would be your relatives. Now they are a source of good memories.

One such memory for me is of a little maple syrup project on the hillside behind the school that we had organized on our own, having fashioned little spouts out of pieces of willow and dug holes in the trees with our knives to get the spout inserted, and having found cans or vessels of one kind or another in which to boil the sap. I'm sure our teacher knew about the project, but he never had any part in it. And it wasn't talked about much; it was one of those great secrets that everybody knew about and hoped to be a participant in. To make it work, we had a very nice system. We rotated in turns during the day to see who could get excused from the room so that you could go out and take care of it. You'd just raise your hand and say you were sick, unless you really wanted to go to the outhouse, and you went out. Then it was your turn to go down and put a little more wood on the fire, or maybe put a little more sap in, or a little water to make up for what you'd taken out. In the end, we had a mixture of ashes, sticks, and leaves, and some little sweetness.

Next came high school in the village, about four miles away. Most of these children had to come to school on horseback or bicycle. I came either in a two-seated top wagon or a sleigh, depending on the season and the weather. That was my first introduction to school busing. It was a very happy experience in that connection.

In those years, life at home was a very open education in itself. It's something that hardly exists anymore. Families living and working together, largely self-sufficient, cutting your own wood for fuel, pumping your own water from the well, hauling your own logs to the sawmill for lumber, raising a full variety of produce and livestock for your own use and for sale, neither working for wages nor hiring anyone, expenses very few, financial concerns centered primarily about enough money to pay the mortgage, to pay taxes, and to pay insurance. Beyond that you could get along with almost nothing. No electricity, no telephones, no paved roads, no plumbing, no engines. Neighbors helped one another if a job was too big for your family to do it.

To a child, those days were worry-free. It seemed an endless succession of exciting, satisfying activity with all its joys and sadnesses, and you expected to die there. Sports and recreation were simple and homemade. Square dancing, singing, strawberry festivals, holiday celebrations, visiting neighbors and friends, and once each summer, an all-day expedition to Lake Erie some eight miles away, with its beautiful sand and crystal-clear water and all of its small summer cottages. I think of those years as open education at its best. Now that they're gone, I don't know how we can possibly duplicate them; we have to think of other ways.

After high school, I was offered a job teaching in a one-room school in a neighboring district. My only objective qualifications were that I had a high school diploma. But I'd been a pupil in such a school for eight years and I was willing. When the offer was made to me and I heard that I would be paid $30 a week—which was so many times greater than what I could earn raising corn and potatoes—I jumped at the chance.

Then, after I had worked as a teacher for awhile, I joined a work-study program initiated at Antioch College by Arthur Morgan. More than half of each year was occupied with work away from the college, but under its auspices. This, too, was tremendously stimulating and expanding and open. Let me just mention the job experiences I had in those few years: Ford Motors in Detroit; New Jersey State Institution for Feeble-Minded Males; a wheat field in North Dakota; Frigidaire Corporation, promoting electric refrigerators to replace ice-boxes. My last job at Antioch, as an apprentice teacher, was at the Park School of Buffalo. This was my first contact with a nonpublic country day school. It was the early days of progressive education, and progressive education was the rage then for country day schools. The vitality and the maturity and joy I observed at the Park School were truly thrilling.

During my last term at Antioch, John Dewey gave a series of lectures at Ohio State University that I received permission to attend. The auditorium was crowded, there were no loudspeakers, it was quite difficult to hear him, and, in a sense, even more difficult to understand him. Nevertheless, Dewey's philosophy came through rather strong and clear, stressing interest and activity, with learning related to actual life experiences, and he became from then on, a compelling inspiration in my own life. Before the end of that year I was engaged to teach at an international school in Paris with the hope that I might bring progressive education principles and practices to that school. Although I had had two summers as a camp counselor in Connecticut—one of the first great open summer programs for youngsters, where children participated in all the planning and action—I was about as well qualified for that as I was teaching at the little rural school. Then, returning from France, I started to teach in one of the Associated Experimental Schools in New York City.

There were six schools. They are still in existence. They

were to some degree an offshoot of progressive education, somewhat more oriented toward social and political concerns, rather than merely providing activities and interesting projects for youngsters, and it was a highly stimulating venture in many ways. It was during those years that I pursued my graduate studies at Teachers College, where the professors included Dewey's most ardent disciples and where occasionally Dewey would appear, too, to sympathize with us.

The most exciting event in those years, however, was meeting a teacher from the Bureau of Educational Experiments, better known now as the Bank Street College of Education. That led to Camp Treetops in Lake Placid, where I was married. Camp Treetops, which Helen Douglas Haskell founded, was an even more open place than any I'd experienced before. My first strong impression was the morning council, where the counselor and the children would gather outdoors to make plans for the day, recording endeavors and adventures of the previous day, along with discussions of many common interests. Jobs were planned, problems discussed, and solutions agreed upon. "What happened to the tools taken out on the trail?" "Whose turn was it to weed the garden, harvest the vegetables, wash the dishes, do the barn chores?" Then came the more enticing choices: dancing, making music, practicing for a play, working with clay, weaving, woodwork, science, mountain climbing, swimming, riding, canoeing, sailing, ballgames, exploring the swamp, building a treehouse, playing in the brook. An incredible array of enterprise and activities that no child could possibly feel sorry about. It never ceases to be a source of amazement to me that children not only made their own thoughtful choices, but somehow they remembered most of the choices made by others in the group. You'd ask one child what another was doing that very minute and he'd say, "Oh, Jenny's here or Jenny's there." They were aware of the full organization of the day.

It was at this camp that the idea of a resident school began to take shape. Five years later, in 1938, my wife and I did our best to combine all of these background experiences that I've been relating to make a place where children could live fulltime and also be at school. The idea grew partly from noticing how much more enthusiastic and happy, natural and productive the children were in the freedom and openness of summer camps like the ones where we had worked. In addition, we drew from the best, most progressive, city or country day schools, public or private, that we knew. We combined work and farm programs with self-sufficiency, working with gardens, farm animals, in fields, forests, with much time for art, handcrafts, and music, free play, noncompetitive sports, contact with wilderness, hours of each day out-of-doors, all seasons, all weather, mountains, forests, rivers, streams, lakes, swamps, open fields, seemingly endless space, bordering on three million acres of the Adirondack Forest Preserve. We lived together in small groups. Each group was composed of a family and about eight children. In addition to the many influences already mentioned, we concentrated on giving children more responsibility for their own activities. How can they become more resourceful, reliable people unless they have abundant opportunity to assume responsibility for decisions and actions without close supervision and direction.

When you mention a boarding school for children—since they are so rare indeed—one reaction is that people imagine the students to come mostly from broken homes or are children with emotional or learning problems. Well, we had our share of those children, as all schools should and do. But happily, most of the children came from typical urban or suburban homes. These parents wanted their children to have as broad a range of outdoor country life and country childhood fun as possible—more than they could possibly provide in their own homes, schools, or communities. Many of these parents were in professions or business that allowed too little contact with their own children. One important element was living and working with families—mother, father, and little children—there at the school, where they had as much contact with males as with females. A rare experience for many of our children and an important element in open education.

The concept of open education is valid and vital. It could become a critical element in the natural, logical, maturing of our educational procedures. I think it did develop and mature in this tiny little school up in the mountains. I remember we once had a letter addressed to "The Little School in the Woods." We were, in many respects, "in the woods," following on untrodden paths, trying to find ways to make life exciting and rewarding where children and adults live together.

VINCENT WRIGHT • I really could zero in on a lot of what Mr. Clark said because I think the philosophy of his residential program is pretty much like the philosophy of the Encampment for Citizenship. The encampment is more limited in that it is a six weeks' summer program, but in the six years that I've been involved with the encampment those six weeks are six weeks that the participants never forget.

The encampment was started in 1946, by two people connected with the Ethical Culture Society: Algernon Black, who was active in New York City public affairs for many years until he retired, and Alice Pollitzer, who died two years ago at the age of 102. It started originally as a program for college students, but when we discovered that kids these days mature earlier than we'd given them credit for, we shifted our focus to a high school program. The program, moreover, is not primarily for minority youngsters, because one of the program's basic tenets is cultural pluralism. Therefore, the young people who come to the encampments are drawn from a very diverse background. We look for diversity in these areas: ethnic, religious, racial, economic, and geographic. So what we generally wind up with is anywhere between 75 and 100 students, most of whom are black or white, some of whom are Chicano, or Puerto Rican, or Native American, and all of whom represent a variety of religions. Last summer, we had three young people from Hawaii and two from Guam.

Our aim is to do in six weeks with young people what America has tried to do, and hasn't done too well, which is to get people—its nation of immigrants, as President Franklin Roosevelt said—to come together and recognize their common humanity. Not to change the differences—I think the differences are valuable—but to learn to live with each other and to learn something about each other's culture. Not to use difference as a barrier, but to use it as a bridge. That's one of the focuses—the focus on pluralism.

The other focus is on the philosophy of John Dewey—learning by doing. There are generally four encampments during the summer, in different parts of the country, according to where there is a specific problem with regard to the makeup of the people in the community. (Since I've been involved, we've had encampments in Alabama, Kentucky, Colorado, Texas, and Arizona.) At each of these places, we will have, say, five workshops. For instance, there will be one in educational reform, one in community organization, one in health services, one in ecology and environment, and one on penal reform and criminal justice. The staff arrives at the encampment a week before the students get there and goes out into the community to unearth every possible resource that may be of use to the students in their particular concentration. They'll explore these resources and come back with a whole pile of names, addresses, names of projects, and names of other people who have other projects. Each member of the staff does this. When, a week later, the encampers arrive, the staff members get up and do a selling job. "This is what my workshop is going to do." Then the encampers choose the workshop in which they want to be involved. At that point, the staff member dumps all of the resources into the laps of the encampers, who then decide how they are going to structure their encampment.

The third focus is on having the encampers create and structure their own mini-community, their own government. They make virtually all the rules, the exception being that they will make no rules that violates a federal, state, or city law. And there is a special emphasis on our part that they will not violate any regulation with regard to alcohol or drugs. (My position on drugs is much more a political than a medical one, although I don't smoke cigarettes of any kind and I don't use any drugs.)

The work projects will be held all day Monday, all day Wednesday, and all day Friday. On Tuesday and Thursday, the workshop leader will try to put into some perspective the workshop activities of Monday, Wednesday, and Friday. In addition to that, there are government meetings where the students, as I said, make the rules and regulations, and if necessary enforce any regulations that need to be enforced. It is really a very heavy load for teenagers. It's one thing to make personal decisions, but another to assume collective responsibility. At the encampment, we are not only 75 to 100 individuals, we are also a community. You may make a personal decision, but if that decision negatively affects your community, then you have to think it through again in terms of this collective responsibility.

So the first week is structured by the staff. After that these youngsters have as much activity as they want to get involved in. They also make decisions quite often about the recreation they will take, the speakers they will bring in, the field trips they want to be involved in. In the community government, the staff functions as one vote. In all honesty, I must say that when a staff member says something it does carry more weight because of the fact that the staff member has had more responsibility. But the staff's responsibility then is to sit back and ask questions. Our function is not only to say, when we see them heading towards a mistake, "Don't do it," but—provided it's not too horrendous a mistake—to let them make that mistake. I think we learn from our mistakes, as well. So for six weeks these young people are involved with these work projects, and I must say that some of them are fascinating.

Last summer, some of the encampers in the health workshop composed a fantastic questionnaire on venereal disease. Then they literally went up to people in the street and asked them the questions. It was interesting to discover, if we hadn't known it before, that some people feel that venereal disease doesn't belong to certain social classes. Many people were really taken aback by students asking them about it. But they did, and now the questionnaire is being used in Denver, which is where we were encamped at the time. Likewise, we did a questionnaire on the potential use of bicycles, not as a source of recreation but as a resource of transportation in Denver. As a result of our work, Denver now has bike lanes that are not open to automobile traffic.

I think this is a terribly meaningful program. The problem with it, of course, is that it is only six weeks long. But as I said, I think that those six weeks stay with the kids for a long period afterwards. We have some distinguished alumni, including Eleanor Holmes Norton, Simeon Golar, William Haddad, and Allard Lowenstein. We like to think, of course, that they would never be who they are today if it were not for the encampment. Possibly that works both ways. Like many other individual programs now, the encampment is having serious financial difficulties. The federal money that we used to get does not come so readily anymore. We resist being less independent than we are because we feel that the loss of that independence will make restrictions that will choke us.

Both speakers seem to have talked about the fallacy of separating education from real life. You both described educational experiences that are experiences of living. I wonder if you could comment on how realistic it is to think about establishing the experiences and relationships of a residential school in a day school. I have in mind, specifically, the example of Summerhill. When Summerhill's idea took root many years ago, and people were starting schools in imitation of it, A.S. Neill, in one of his letters, said, "The notion of a Summerhill day school is a contradiction in terms. Summerhill is a way of life that goes on 24 hours a day." To take a child out of a surburban home where he was close to television and all kinds of immediate influences, and so on, and put him into a so-called Summerhill day school for five hours a day, seems difficult, to say the least. I wonder if either of you have any comment on that issue?

CLARK ● I indicated, near the end of my remarks, that the only way I can see the residential idea working in day schools would be under a much different organization than now exists. Most of our day schools are organized for a very prescribed area. They don't concern themselves very much with what lies outside of that sphere. It's hard to go further with that structure. It seems to me that all the teaching aides in the world have done nothing. To begin to change that, parents almost have to be required to become more involved again. Obviously you can't require anybody to do anything if you want him to do it well. But if parents would be more—much more—involved than they are in the day school situation, there could be a new approach to what we call open. We could have all sorts of adults coming into the schools.

Parents care a lot about their children; they want them to be well educated, but they don't realize how much they can learn, and I don't see anybody giving them the chance to learn.

WRIGHT • My answer might be a bit cynical, in terms of whether there is hope or not under the present structure. I think we need to talk about what we are educating our kids for. I was on a panel a couple of years ago at a high school in East Meadow, Long Island, and a young man said, he lies and cheats and steals and would do anything to get those grades because he knows that's what is expected of him. And a parent got up to make the most incredible remark I've ever heard in my life. Agreeing with the young man, she said, "The world of work out there is very tough and it's a very competitive society." In effect, what she was supporting was the old Richard Nixon philosophy of living: the worst thing about cheating is getting caught.

On the one hand, we become extremely judgmental when kids do poorly in mathematics, even though most normal people only use up to sixth grade arithmetic in their everyday lives. On the other hand, how much energy have we expended toward making people learn how to make it together? Let's face it, the days of being closed off to one another are finished: We *are* going to meet our brothers and sisters. The question is, are we going to meet them with guns and knives or are we going to meet them with friendship and understanding.

What strikes me about openness in schools, about the schools that I think do work, is not only the dedication of the people involved, the commitment and the belief in what they're doing, but the sense of community, the sense of a center—working toward a common purpose. That was the essential plan for these residential schools, where they had the community thing: living together and struggling and becoming dependent upon one another. That doesn't occur in what we call public schools. I think that stems somewhat from the kind of training people get when they go into those schools. I was struck by it because I'm now working in an institution that trains teachers in probably a different way from most. The whole core of our program is one that stresses group life and group values for children. But it's a hard thing to bring about, especially if you are alone as a teacher. A lot of teachers have trouble when they go into groups, when they go into public settings. Their values are lost. They have to make a life out of their life knowledge, out of what they are, and the value in which they hold themselves is very often turned off in the schools, perhaps against their will.

WRIGHT • That really strikes a responsive note in me. I think that teaching is one of the most important, if not the most important, profession in this society. I remember a few years ago reading about a woman who got up at a Board of Estimate meeting and said that she was an immigrant and grateful to be in this country, but what she didn't understand, when they were talking about cutting funds for education, is how such a great country ignores its future, because the kids are what the future is. This may sound awful, but I think that a lot of people who are in teaching hate children. I think that teaching has two components. First, one has to have a unique body of knowledge that you're going to pass on to other people. But it's the other component that is often ignored: How are you going to pass that body of knowledge on to the other one, what method do you use, and what do you think about the people that you're passing it on to? Do you teach courses or do you teach people? I've been teaching for 15 years now. I started teaching in the public school system after having had education courses, but the first day I learned anything about teaching was in the classroom because my education courses prepared me to teach in Mars somewhere. I think that we need to seriously reevaluate not only the educational priorities but who is teaching.

My question has to do with interdependence being harder than independence. What both of you suggest, and what people have said here today, seems to be that in residential settings the interdependence becomes a very important factor in the learning process, something that is much easier to get at in a residential setting than in a public school setting. You get children who have been "educated" in the public school system. Since the process they've learned seems to be counter to the kinds of things you want to do, what problems do you find in reeducating them and how do you do that?

WRIGHT ● It is a very difficult process, and I think you're absolutely right, that the kids come there feeling that this question of collective responsibility is very difficult. We had a problem last summer when some kids were smoking pot. So we got the community together, and in my anger, I said, "Unless this community deals with this, I'm going to deal with it in a very establishment way, because my feeling is that you are really jeopardizing your brothers and sisters in this community. Not only that, you're jeopardizing future encampments." To deal with it, they chose a very humane way, which I didn't think would work. One young woman from Montana said, "I think we ought to sit in this room until that person who has been using it confesses." We sat in that room for 23 hours until the person responsible finally stood up and confessed. Time wasted, but a great learning experience. It made them recognize that the action of just one person was jeopardizing everyone else. Finally, the guilt which that person felt for jeopardizing his brothers and sisters made him confess to it. They embraced him and he told them how sorry he was. I think that it is very difficult to learn interdependence, but we are all, in this universe, dependent on each other in some way.

A View of School Reform

VITO PERRONE • At what point does one seek roots? Generally, what we've come to learn, is that such a need occurs quite naturally, at times of crisis, during periods of consolidation, when an individual is moving from one stage of maturing life to another. In like fashion, there are times when individuals, who are struggling to make schools—as well as families and neighborhoods—more responsive to the developmental needs of children and young people, feel they are alone and reach out for connection.

In doing just that today, many of us have found—as others have known all along—that this important struggle has been in process for decades, supported by large, and growing, numbers of people in many parts of the country. So it is both natural and useful to take time out from the daily practice to make a study of some of the historical philosophical roots of open education, especially to permit those of us who are involved to reflect more seriously on our efforts.

My point of departure is the decade following 1840, a time of revolutionary upheaval in Europe and the years preceding the Civil War in the United States. The focus on the 1840s is not meant to suggest that schooling was not an important element in American life prior to that time but it is in *that* period that a serious commitment to universal education was made.[1] (Such a commitment is basic, I should add, to much of what open education is about.)

Horace Mann in Massachusetts, Henry Barnard in Connecticut, and John D. Pierce in Michigan were the early evangelists for universal education, the establishment of schools where, to paraphrase the sentiment of the day, "all of America's children could meet, where democratic life could be nurtured, strong character built and economic and cultural growth guaranteed." It is relatively easy today to ascribe class biases to Mann, Barnard, and Pierce, to suggest that their powerful sermons about the "needs of children" were in fact just sermons, especially in light of what the common schools became. But I don't believe they must bear the full burden for the "sins of their sons."[2] Their preaching helped bring significant results; school systems providing elementary education began to take shape across the country. As the schools grew in number, they also became, to a large degree, more systematized and formal. Graded patterns, which we know so well, became the norm by 1870. In order to accommodate the graded classification of students, subject matter—such as first-, second-, and third-grade readers—became graded. Covering the graded materials became a dominant theme in schools. Memorization took up much of a child's time. The textbooks were encyclopedic and not particularly adapted to the interests of children. The language of the factory, slowly becoming a dominant force in the American economy of the 19th century, became the language of the schools.[3] We still live, unfortunately, with the school-as-factory metaphor. The consequences of it are profound.

Dropouts were high in the common schools throughout the 19th century. And in spite of the best hopes of egalitarians such as Mann, the common schools served, especially in the East, mostly the poor and lower middle classes (with blacks generally excluded). The upper middle and wealthy classes patronized private scools, as they had in the pre-Civil War period. Secondary schools came later, beginning to replace the academies after 1870. They tended to be academic/college preparatory in character and served a very small number of students. Even by the close of the century, in spite of some growing interest in broadening the secondary curriculum to include vocational subjects and support large numbers of youngsters from less advantaged populations, the secondary schools attracted very few young people from working class or newly-arrived immigrant families. The secondary schools did not serve such groups to any significant degree until the 1920s and 1930s. And a case could be made to the effect that the schools still do not serve such groups.

A View of School Reform

In 1900, only about 8 percent of the young people of secondary school age—post-eighth grade—were actually attending a secondary school. To gain some further perspective on how far schools have come in relation to the idea of universal education, it might be of interest to look at some statistics from North Dakota, a not untypical rural state, shortly after the turn of the century. Of the children entering the first grade, approximately 50 percent remained for the second grade, about 25 percent continued to the eighth grade, and 1.5 percent completed high school.[4]

In general, the schools of the 19th century, especially in their practice, were bleak. It is impossible, however, to read the literature of the period without recognizing the enormous problems with which school people had to contend: fiscal support was inadequate, school facilities could not be built rapidly enough to take care of the numbers of children who wished to attend. Precedents for mass schooling were not readily available. And the social order was in a state of rapid transition, especially in the urban areas. (Urban population, for example, increased from 9.9 million in 1870 to 30.1 million in 1900.) But the bleakness did not go totally unchallenged, and this is important to understand. The seriousness of the challenge becomes clear as one reads the accounts. And for that reason alone, if for no other, reading the literature is of value. Michael Katz, who has provided us with some critical revisionist perspectives on American education, acknowledges that the 19th century debates about schools, their organizational patterns and instructional practices, were intense and often thoughtful. (He is generally less positive about the quality of contemporary debate.)[5]

After his election to the Boston School Committee in 1879, the historian Brooks Adams wrote in an essay for the *Atlantic* that:

> The aim now is to excite children to enthusiasm for knowledge, not to continue to deaden the mind with the old system of lockstep procedure and memorization. Knowing that you cannot teach a child everything, it is best to teach a child how to learn.[6]

In reaction to the growing centralization of the school district, a colleague on the Boston board suggested that ritual and routine was drawing a wedge between teacher and pupil, altering what had been a more meaningful relationship. . . . The no-system plan (decentralization) was far more conducive to developing individuality and character.[7]

These two forms of argument arose often in the 19th century literature. They arise today. They will undoubtedly arise in the future. But unless we become more effective in building substance into our work or in giving increased levels of support to parents, teachers, and school administrators who are engaged in a process of educational reexamination, these will continue, as they were then, to be minority positions.

An important 19th century American progressive reformer was Francis W. Parker, referred to by John Dewey as the "Father of Progressive Education." In 1873, after considerable travel in Europe—Holland, Germany, Switzerland, Italy, and France—where educational reform was particularly active, Parker accepted the position of Superintendent of the Quincy, Massachusetts, schools with a mandate for "substantial" change. And change did come. For large numbers of teachers, enthusiasm for teaching was revived. The linear, lockstep curriculum was abandoned along with the traditional reader and speller. Materials developed by teachers, along with local newspapers and magazines, were introduced as a base for expanding the curriculum. Field trips into the local community became common—a base for geography and local history. Manipulative devices came into increasing use in arithmetic. "The child and his needs" became the focus of attention.

In response to some of his critics who thought the Quincy schools were abandoning reading, writing, and arithmetic and "experimenting with children," Parker wrote in his report to the School Committee in 1879:

> I am simply trying to apply well-established principles of teaching . . . the methods springing from them are found in the development of every child. They are used everywhere except in school. . . . No experiments have been tried.[8]

How many of you here at this conference have said the same thing in relation to your own work?

A View of School Reform

Parker's efforts attracted considerable attention. Visitors came from throughout the United States as well as Europe to visit Parker and the Quincy schools. In 1882, Parker went on to the principalship of the Cook County Normal and Practice School in Chicago, where he was influential in furthering child-centered practices. His *Talks on Pedagogics,* published in 1894, while Victorian in style, encouraged many teachers to make fresh beginnings. As the 19th century drew to a close, proposals to focus on *the child* rather than on *subject matter* came from many sources, outside as well as inside of the organized educational establishment.

One such important source was the settlement house movement. The range of activities engaged in by the settlement houses was large. Their agenda included active campaigning for improved housing, child labor laws, neighborhood recreational facilities, and provisions for medical care (they campaigned for national health insurance as early as 1910). In addition to struggling for the construction of increased numbers of elementary schools, leaders in the settlement houses called for a different kind of education, one that concerned itself with children's physical and social well-being along with their intellectual growth. Many of the settlement houses organized cooperative nurseries, conducted kindergarten programs, and provided a variety of opportunities for intergenerational learning. They tended to view the school as having an integral relationship to their efforts at improving the quality of community life. Jane Addams, director of Hull House in Chicago, used the phrase "socialized education" for the forms she advocated.[9]

While the settlement houses gave encouragement to many immigrants, immigrant groups themselves also organized successfully in many parts of the country to preserve their cultural roots, in large measure through a host of informal learning activities. I am most familiar with the Italian-American Societies, but almost every immigrant group organized in similar ways. These groups constantly drew from their life experiences and older cultural patterns as guides for sustaining their individuality and for giving to their children the support that the schools were generally unprepared to provide. Their influence on the formal schools was never large, but I believe that we all have something to learn from them. That so many immigrants survived, maintaining their spirit, is a tribute to their internal resources and the power of their informal learning patterns. I think of my own immigrant father in relation to this. It is unfortunate that the schools did not draw on his life experience. He never set foot in a school in his native Italy, coming to America as an illiterate at the age of 18. By the time he was 25, without access to any educational system or institutional tutoring program, he had become literate in English, so powerful was his drive to learn. He read and wrote very well, gaining enormous support for his learning over the years within the confines of his family, a natural learning base.

In the rural areas of the country, especially as rural population began to level off or decline, concerns were raised about transforming the schools into community centers that would play a role in revitalizing the quality of rural life and provide more practical and stimulating experiences for children. As Liberty Hyde Bailey wrote, "I want to see our country schools without screwed-down seats and to see children put to work with tools and soils and plants and problems."[10] Bailey, as Dean of Agriculture at Cornell, actively promoted a more natural curriculum, with a community-building orientation that had as its starting point what he called "Nature Study." Cornell turned out lively curriculum materials and progressive philosophy through the first two decades of the 20th century.

The influence of the Country Life Movement was profound. While it was parochial, the Country Life Movement had substance. Schooling took on a larger significance in many parts of rural America. Formalism began to decline. And traditions were built in many rural communities that, even today, provide a healthy soil for the serious reexamination that open education demands.[11] Many individuals who came out of America's rural schools continue today to provide significant leadership to open education practice. In acknowledging Marian Brooks's contribution, we honor one such individual today.

Another individual who provided impetus for progressivism in schools in the 1890s was Joseph Meyer Rice. Trained as a pediatrician, Rice became sufficiently concerned about school practice to undertake, on behalf of the *Forum,* a leading opinion journal of the period, a status study of American education. His report, which ran in nine issues of the *Forum* between October 1892 and June 1893, was a bombshell. Rice argued that "in city after city, public apathy, political interference, corruption and incompetence were conspiring to ruin the schools.... With alarming frequency the story was the same: political hacks hiring untrained teachers who blindly led their innocent charges in singsong drill, rote repetition, and meaningless verbiage."[12]

In addition to his sharp critique, Rice called attention to a number of examples of what he termed "progressive" practice in such communities as Minneapolis, Indianapolis, Chicago, and LaPorte (Indiana). Parker's Practice School received his most enthusiastic response. Rice's report became a matter of widespread discussion providing, as Lawrence Cremin has suggested, sufficient self-consciousness among educational reformers to give shape to an active progressive education movement. I might add that the *Forum* during the decade of the 1890s carried a number of interesting descriptions of schools. I was particularly engrossed recently in a September 1894 article by Mary Laing, entitled "Child Study: A Teacher's Record of Her Pupils," which described exemplary practice in the Froebel Academy of Brooklyn, organized originally in 1884. Persons involved in open education would find it particularly instructive.

John Dewey, more than any other person, gave the reform movement intellectual leadership.[13] Through his writings, he continues to provide inspiration to those who seek more progressive practice in schools. In 1896, Dewey, his wife Alice, and several neighbors in Chicago began a Laboratory School to put into practice some of the educational theory that Dewey had been formulating. The school, more commonly called The Dewey School, opened with 16 children and two teachers; by 1902, it had 140 childern, 23 regular teachers, and 10 assistants who were University of Chicago graduate students. While its life was relatively short, closing in 1904, the school had a long enough history to help Dewey consolidate his educational theory. Unfortunately, it was the last intensive relationship Dewey had with a school. Had he continued such a relationship during his Columbia years, the synthesis in his thinking that characterized his later life—a reconciliation between "heart and mind," a further softening of his faith in science—might have come earlier. And had he remained active in schools, he might have provided during his very active life the serious linking of theory and practice that progressive education seemed to lack at critical times, such as during the Depression years.

School and Society, which contained Dewey's lectures to parents connected with the Laboratory School, provides an early view of Dewey's educational thought. He emphasized the need for active learning and a conception of the school as a community, "active with types of occupations that reflect the life of the larger society, and permeated throughout with the spirit of art, history and science."[14]

It is unfortunate that what occurred—the practice—in the Laboratory School was not more available in the literature of the early progressive period. This becomes clear as one reads *The Dewey School: The Laboratory School of the University of Chicago 1896-1903,* written by Katherine Camp Mayhew and Anna Camp Edwards, sisters who taught in the school.[15] Their accounts, drawn from the careful records that were maintained, describe what may well have been progressive education at its best. Had the descriptions been available before 1910, progressive education practice might well have developed more successfully.

In *Schools for Tomorrow,* published in 1915, Dewey presented his educational views in a very direct fashion, suggesting that American education was characterized by a lack of democratic practice. In addition to summarizing his philosophy, he described (along with his daughter, Evelyn) schools in many parts of the country that were attempting to implement progressive practice. Among the schools that Dewey highlighted was the School for Organic Education in Fairhope, Alabama. Begun in 1907 by Marietta Johnson, who was to occupy one of the hallowed niches of progressive education, the school remains intact to this day. Recently I read Marietta Johnson's *Thirty Years With an Idea*—published during the past year—and found her educational transforma-

A View of School Reform

tion quite similar to that of many young teachers with whom I work today.[16] She came from my neighboring state of Minnesota and taught for several years in St. Paul. At one point, she asked her superintendent why the school programs had so little relation to children's growth. His response—to paraphrase it—was, "Isn't it disgraceful that they don't?" Shortly thereafter, Marietta Johnson decided to begin a school. She was a woman with deep insights into learning. She was also full of bravado, capable of convincing almost anyone that progressive education was absolutely essential to children's well-being.

In the early years of the 20th century a self-conscious progressivism began to take hold in many schools; for example, the University of Missouri Lab School (1904), Caroline Pratt's Play School in New York City (1913), The Park School in Baltimore (1912), Bryn Mawr Elementary School (1913), the Edgewood School, Greenwich, Connecticut (1913), the Walden School that was organized by Margaret Naumburg in New York City (1915), the Shady Hill School in Cambridge, Massachusetts (1915), the University of Iowa Elementary School (1915), Oak Lane Country Day School in Philadelphia (1916), and the Lincoln School, associated with Teachers College, Columbia (1917), among others. The Ethical Culture Schools, begun in New York City in the 19th century, took on a progressive orientation, as did the Friends Schools, located in a number of eastern cities. The Minneapolis public schools, the Menominee and Milwaukee schools in Wisconsin, and the Winnetka, Illinois, schools, under Carlton Washburne, a product of Francis Parker's Practice School, all organized heavily around progressive principles.[17] Even in classrooms and schools where self-conscious progressivism was not pursued, there was an increasing support for taking the child into account. Formalism began to subside.

The foregoing ought not to suggest that progressive education was "sweeping the country." It wasn't. Ann Shumacher and Harold Rugg, in their 1928 study, report: "The Child-Centered Schools as yet constitute but a corporal's guard as compared with the great regiments of formal schools."[18] On the other hand, there was enough occurring to keep progressivism alive and capable of influencing educational practice in general.

As progressive practice grew, the need for communication increased. It was this motivation, as well as the desire to generate more pressure for reform, that served as the impetus for organizing the Progressive Education Association (PEA) in 1919, the prime mover of which was Stanwood Cobb, who had been introduced to progressivism by Marietta Johnson. Johnson was the major influence in forging the "statement of principles" that was used as a basis for organizing. Charles Eliot, then President of Harvard, accepted the honorary presidency. (What college president today is prepared to endorse progressive principles?) John Dewey, after some reluctance, agreed to accept the honorary presidency after Eliot's death in 1927. From a modest beginning, the Association grew to almost 11,000 members at its height in 1938. It was vigorous and mission-oriented, especially in its early years. Its journal, *Progressive Education,* begun in 1924, was *the* education journal of its day.

The literature flowing from the Progressive Education Association was voluminous—almost too voluminous, as the 1930s came. The careful analysis that characterized the early progressive writing—especially that of Dewey, James and Kilpatrick—gave way to popularization, which created new problems. Almost every new direction in education claimed the umbrella of progressive education, including vocational education, administrative efficiency, professionalization of teachers, standardized testing, and tracking. Given the progressive movement's broad framework in the United States, tied as it was to a strong belief in the virtue of science, this urge for all-inclusiveness was understandable. But for many individuals, such an all-inclusive movement could not be supported. What had begun at the turn of the century as a relatively broad-based reform effort became by 1920 a narrower movement dominated by professional educators in the still burgeoning teachers colleges. The support of the more informal institutions, such as the settlement houses, began to wane. And progressive practice, in its most self-conscious forms, became increasingly more evident in private rather than public schools.

A View of School Reform

Reading the progressive literature of the 1920s and 1930s is interesting for a number of reasons. In particular, it parallels so much of the writing associated with the early phase of open education (1967-71). The language is almost identical. It, too, lacked significant substance in large measure. It tended toward romanticism, to echo Featherstone's discussion presented here earlier. Being deeply involved with open education today, as I am, may color my view of the progressive literature of the 1920s and 1930s much too critically. But, from my perspective, that literature seems far too defensive. There were attacks on traditional forms of education long past the point where such rhetoric was useful. The interplay between theory and practice that was a part of the earlier progressive formulations seems stale by comparison, especially in the 1930s. Documentation of good practice was limited. Evaluation processes were not very well developed. Self-criticism was limited. Harold Rugg suggested that: "Teachers have not become students—either of society, of child needs or curriculum construction."[19] The literature seems to support Rugg's conclusion. But, it should also be noted, I found little in the literature that suggested organized support for the growth of teachers as significant learners.

The Depression, coming as it did, undoubtedly affected progressivism in the schools. The economic collapse was so severe that the problems of schools paled by comparison. With the Depression, the literature tended to take on a society-centered, in contrast to a child-centered, focus. The major progressive debate of the 1930s related to how, or whether, the schools should respond to the economic and social crisis. Ideological debate slowly began to take its toll on the progressive movement. George Counts, in his "Dare Progressive Education Be Progressive,"[20] focused on the need for the schools to take a central role in the reconstruction of the American society. Counts believed, as did others, that progressivism was losing its vitality because it was focusing too much attention on "techniques of instruction" and not enough on its "social and political obligations." While the discussions were certainly lively—to read the *Social Frontier*, a progressive journal that George Counts edited during its most controversial period, is an exciting endeavor—it seems clear in retrospect that the ideological arguments were going nowhere. A more modest view of schools and schooling would have helped at the time, as it would now.

By the 1930s, with much of the fervor of earlier years waning, the PEA succumbed to establishing commissions for every concern or question raised—clearly an academic rather than activist response. It took few stands on such issues as inequality in schools, racial segregation, testing and tracking, and problems in the social composition of school boards.

The Progressive Education Association never recovered its stride, even after World War II. While the rhetoric remained intact—individualization, student initiative, integrated learning, creative self-expression, maximum growth of the child, spontaneity, community—it seemed increasingly less rooted in practice. The practice that existed appears to have plateaued. Between 1942-1946, Harold Rugg revisited many of the progressive schools that had been part of his study during the 1920s. While he was impressed by much that existed, he also expressed discomfort:

> Something seemed to be missing from these schools. I noticed it first in their social studies. A strange aloofness from society seemed to mark them. . . . My visits left me with the definite impression that the schools were doing little more than they had done in the 1920s; that they were still describing the community, the nation and the modern world. They seemed afraid of forthright realistic dealing with the actual conditions of their local communities. Certainly they dodged most of the controversial issues of the day. I found less interest in the creative and appreciative act in the Progressive schools than in 1927 when I was writing *The Child Centered School*.[21]

"Life Adjustment Education," especially in relation to the secondary schools, was part of the postwar progressive ideology. Poorly defined, lacking a theoretical base (certainly far removed from Dewey's concept of community) or operational construct, it floundered. "Progressive Education" was no longer popular. Historian Arthur Bestor, a graduate of the progressive Lincoln School, among others, led a series of attacks on postwar progressivism. His *Educational Wastelands* (1953) was a particularly harsh statement, describing "life adjustment" education as a "retreat from learning." Schools were on the defensive to an almost unprecedented degree. In 1955, the Progressive Education Association went out of existence and the *Progressive Educational Journal,* long past its vital period, collapsed two years later. In closing his work on the progressive education movement, Lawrence Cremin writes:

> The Progressive Education Association had died, and progessive education itself needed drastic reappraisal. Yet the transformation they had wrought in the schools was in many ways as irreversible as the larger industrial transformation of which it had been a part. And for all the talk about pedagogical breakthroughs and crash programs, the authentic progressive view remained strangely pertinent to the problems of midcentury America. Perhaps it only awaited the reformulation and resuscitation that would ultimately derive from a larger resurgence of reform in American life and thought.[22]

Before ending the discussion of the Progressive Education Association altogether, I should call attention to its Eight-Year Study. The study involved 1,475 graduates of 30 progressive schools. Completed under the direction of Wilford Aiken in 1940, the results were published in 1942. Had the nation not been at war, the study might have received greater attention. It deserves rereading by those who wish to understand the period.[23] Did the graduates of progressive schools succeed in college? The results were far more positive than the most ardent progressives expected. Matched person for person, the graduates of the progressive schools tended to outdistance their nonprogressive school peers on almost all of the academic and social dimensions studied.

While progressive education as a self-conscious movement was dead by the time of Sputnik, Sputnik led to an increase in the level of criticism of the schools and their "softness," the reaction to which was a heavy infusion of new federal dollars, massive curriculum projects led by university scholars, and a retreat from much that had been learned about learning. While it may be too early to assess this effort in any definitive manner, it seems clear that it achieved—outside of some of the process efforts in elementary science and math—very limited success, if that. By bypassing teachers, by failing to take children's learning processes into sufficient account, and by removing curriculum even further from the communities that nurture schools, the effort had little chance to succeed.[24]

Cremin's comment, that "Perhaps [progressivism in education] only awaited the reformulation . . . that would ultimately derive from a larger resurgence of reform in American life and thought," may well have been prophetic. The 1960s brought about a major social revolution in the United States: the Civil Rights movement, which had gained in momentum in the latter years of the 1950s, became a fulcrum for social and political reform. The inequities in American life became increasingly apparent. The failure of the education system to provide quality schooling on an equal basis to all Americans became a potent issue. Support for pluralism, long cast aside in the wake of "melting pot" theory, won recognition as the necessary base for the creation of social democracy. Depersonalization of life, created in part by increasing levels of technology and bureaucratization in all phases of mainstream American society, brought a radical reaction. The rapid destruction of our natural resources encouraged an increased concern for "spaceship earth." And the war in Vietnam, which proved to be more unpopular than any previous U.S. military involvement, brought protest to a high level. It is against this backdrop that open education as a large-scale movement began building on much that was basic to progressive education.

While drawing heavily upon older progressive sources, the current practice of open education also gained considerable stimulus from England and its primary schools. But inasmuch as that history may be more common than what I have been discussing, I will not pursue it at this time.

In this time of seeking roots, we could do much more. There still remains a need for good description of particular schools, some sense of what caused them to begin, and the factors that led to their alteration of direction. The influence of politics—local, state, and national—on more progressive educational directions needs also to be understood better. In spite of Mann's admonition of the 1840s that schools should take on a neutral value orientation, and educators' long denial that schools are political institutions, it is clear that politics have played a significant role.

There are clearly some differences in the present open education movement in comparison to past progressive efforts. Let me enumerate some. A theoretical base is now more solid. Piaget, in particular, has been responsible for much of this. Open education is more rooted in public education than was progressive education. A higher degree of self-conscious documentation is beginning to occur—practitioners are beginning to explicate what they are about. Their language is growing in specificity. "Community" as a geographic and social construct is being affirmed. It hardly got off the ground in earlier years.

To read the history of American education is to come across large numbers of people who have struggled to make schools responsive to children and young people, to make them more humane and sensitive. It needs to be said further that reform efforts in American education have always had the dubious legacy of being compared to some "idealized past." The past, especially in relation to schooling, is not ideal. The myth that "schools once *taught* reading and other basic skills," and the obvious implication that they *now* don't, for example, is not capable of being sustained by the evidence that exists. A serious reading of the history of American education makes that clear. There are many other myths that need examination. Not to examine them seriously will keep reform efforts on the defensive to some degree, having to prove themselves in ways not required of more conventional forms of education.

The earlier progressives, John Dewey among them, didn't have an adequate perspective on the history of reform. Those of us who are involved with more open processes of education suffer from a similar shortcoming. It would be easy enough, given the "recession" in education, to withdraw from efforts to make schools more responsive to children, to negate what is being learned in the process of educational reexamination and more open processes of education, to "go back to the basics," a current euphemism for conservative reaction in education, as well as in the arenas of economics, social welfare, and civil rights. Fortunately, the commitments are larger than that. While I don't foresee a time soon when schools will be, on a massive scale, as responsive as they *could be,* "decent schools," to use Joseph Featherstone's phrase, are increasing. The progressives' hopes, revived with the advent of open education, are still alive.

References

1. Lawrence Cremin begins his classic history of progressive education, *The Transformation of the School* (New York: Alfred Knopf, 1961), with the pre-Civil War debate about universal education.
2. Horace Mann and the other reformers of his day hardly envisioned the kinds of rigid school systems that developed. While Mann felt that it was necessary to systematize the schools in order to assure access for all children and some measure of standard quality, he expected teachers and administrators to be responsive to children, taking children's interests seriously, supporting individuality. *The Life and Works of Horace Mann,* 5 volumes (Boston: Lee and Shepard, 1891), contain most of Mann's educational writings. An interesting recent biography is by Jonathan Messerli, *Horace Mann* (New York: Knopf, 1971).
3. Michael Katz, in *Class, Bureaucracy and the Schools* (New York: Praeger, 1971), a revisionist account of American education, argues that the fundamental structure of American education was pretty much established by 1880 and "has not been altered since in spite of reformist efforts." Richard Pratte makes a similar point in his interesting analysis, *The Public School Movement* (New York: McKay, 1973).
4. Erling N. Rolfsrud, *The Story of North Dakota* (Alexandria, Minnesota: Lantern, 1963), p. 246.
5. In addition to *Class, Bureaucracy and Schools,* see Katz, *The Irony of Early School Reform: Educational Innovation in Mid-Nineteenth Century Massachusetts* (Cambridge: Beacon Press, 1970). Cremin's *Transformation of the Schools* is an invaluable source for understanding the intellectual and moral vigor that has often characterized American education. See also: Merle Curti, *The Growth of American Thought* (New York: Harper and Row, 3rd edition, 1964), Rush Welter, *Popular Education and Democratic Thought in America* (New York: Columbia University Press, 1962), David Tyack, ed., *Turning Points in American Educational History* (Waltham, Massachusetts: Blaisdell, 1967), Joel Spring, *Education and the Rise of the Industrial State* (Boston: Beacon Press, 1972), Colin Greer, *The*

A View of School Reform

Great School Legend (New York: Viking Press, 1972), Edward Krug, *The Shaping of the American High School*, Vol. I (Madison: University of Wisconsin Press, 1964), and Harold Rugg, *Foundations for American Education* (New York: World Book Co., 1947).

6. Arthur Beringause, *Brooks Adams: A Biography* (New York: Knopf, 1955), pp. 66-67.
7. Katz, *Class, Bureaucracy and Schools*, p. 83.
8. Cremin, p. 130.
9. See Allen Davis, *Spearheads for Reform: The Social Settlements and the Progressive Movement, 1890-1914* (New York: Oxford University Press, 1967) and Jane Addams, *Twenty Years at Hull House* (New York: Macmillan, 1910 and reprinted 1966).
10. Liberty Hyde Bailey, *The Country Life Movement in the United States* (New York: World Book Co., 1911).
11. See "A Daring Educational Experiment: The One-Room School House," *New York Times Magazine* (May 30, 1971).
12. Cremin, pp. 4-5.
13. Those wishing to read some syntheses of Dewey's thought might refer to Joseph Ratner, *Intelligence in the Modern World: John Dewey's Philosophy* (New York: Random House, 1939) and Irwin Edman, *John Dewey* (New York: Bobbs and Merrill, 1955). Dewey was a particularly prolific writer, producing 50 books and innumerable articles. The books which had the most profound impact on progressive education are: *School and Society*, originally published in 1899 and reprinted by the University of Chicago Press, 1956; *How We Think*, originally published in 1910 and reprinted by Regnery, 1971; *Schools for Tomorrow* (with his daughter Evelyn), originally published in 1915 and reprinted by Dutton, 1962; *Democracy and Education*, originally published in 1916 and reprinted by Macmillan, 1961; *Experience and Nature* (New York: Macmillan, 1929); *Experience and Education*, originally published in 1938 and reprinted by Macmillan in 1963.
14. Dewey, *School and Society*, p. 29.
15. Published by Appleton-Century-Crofts in 1936. Reprinted by Atherton Press (New York), 1966.
16. *Thirty Years With an Idea* was published by the University of Alabama Press, 1974.
17. See Harold Rugg and Ann Shumacher, *The Child-Centered School: An Approach of the New Education* (New York: World Book Co., 1928) for descriptions of many of the schools listed. Charlotte Winsor, in *Experimental Schools Revisited* (New

York: Agathon Press, 1973), has brought together a number of documents written between 1917-1924 relating to many of the schools listed above.
18. Rugg and Shumacher, p. III.
19. Rugg, *Foundations of American Education*, p. 315.
20. *Progressive Education*, Vol. 9 (1932), pp. 257-263.
21. Rugg, *Foundations of American Education*, pp. 20-21.
22. Cremin, p. 253. In a later book, *The Genius of American Education*, 1965, Cremin argued that Progressivism never came to terms with the educational revolution that was occurring outside the schools, i.e., radio, film, television. He also noted the failure to understand the altering patterns of family life and the impact of urbanization and industrialization. Open education, and the society-at-large, are still struggling with these issues.
23. Five volumes comprise the full study. The entire effort is summarized in the volume by William Aiken, *The Story of the Eight Year Study* (New York: McGraw Hill, 1942).
24. Charles Silberman, *Crisis in the Classroom* (New York: Random House, 1970) and John Goodlad et al., *Behind the Classroom Doors* (Worthington, Ohio: Charles Jones, 1970) argue in a convincing manner that schools changed little in spite of the 1960s rhetoric of innovation.

Bringing in the apple crop, Children's Aid Society at Kensico, New York. Late 1800s. Jacob Riis Collection, Museum of the City of New York.

Building with blocks, L'Ouverture Kindergarten, late 1800s. Susan Blow established the first kindergarten in an American public school in 1873. Association for Childhood Education International.

Bibliography

Compiled by MARIAN BROOKS

AKWESASNE EDUCATION

Akwesasne Notes. Official publication of the Mohawk Nation. Published 5 times a year by Program in American Studies, State University of New York at Buffalo. Address: Mohawk Nation via Rooseveltown, N.Y. 13683.

PRE- AND POST-EMANCIPATION SCHOOLS

Ottley, Roi and Weatherby, W. J. *The Negro in New York: An Informal Social History, 1646-1940.* New York: Praeger, 1967.

WORKERS EDUCATION

Brameld, T. W., ed. *Workers' Education in the U.S.* New York: Harper, 1941. Fifth Yearbook of the John Dewey Society. A good compendium of writings about the labor education movement.

Industrial Education. American Federation of Labor, Washington, D.C., 1910. Labor's early support for vocational education.

Lindley, Betty and Ernest. *A New Deal for Youth.* New York: De Capo Press, 1935. Educational programs offered by the Civilian Conservation Corps. See also: Ray Hoyt. *"We Can Take It": A Short Story of the C.C.C.* New York: American Book Co.

SETTLEMENT HOUSES

Addams, Jane. *Democracy and Social Ethics.* New York: Macmillan, 1902. Her view of "socialized education" as a protest against the school's only stress on reading and writing and its failure to give the child any clues to the life around him. *Twenty Years at Hull House.* New York: Macmillan, 1910 and *The Second Twenty Years at Hull House.* New York: Macmillan, 1930. Both are autobiographical statements of her work and her educational views. And, *Spirit of Youth and the City Streets.* Reprint. Boston: Little Brown Co., 1950.

Hall, Helen. *Unfinished Business.* New York: Macmillan, 1971. A stirring story of one of the most successful settlement houses that has reached out to unite family and community.

Wald, Lillian. *The House on Henry Street.* New York: Dover, 1915. A history that reflects her concern for the health and welfare of all children and her promotion of programs designed to meet these needs.

Woods, Robert and Kennedy, Albert. *The Settlement Horizon.* New York: Arno Press, 1922. Early programs in the American settlement movement.

THE *SHULE*

Most information concerning the Yiddish *Shule* movement—or more accurately, movements, as there have been several concurrent ones—is in Yiddish: Sh. Niger, *Die Geshichte fun die Shuln* (The History of the Yiddish Schools) 1950s. The Sholem Aleichem Folk Institute (3301 Bainbridge Avenue, Bronx, NY 10467) published a history of their schools, *Our First Fifty Years,* edited by Saul Goodman (Yiddish and English). The Educational Committee of the Workmen's Circle (40 East 33 Street, New York City 10016) published a history of that fraternal organization that includes material concerning Workmen's Circle Schools, *The Friendly Societies,* by Dr. Judah Shapiro (English). Philadelphia Workmen's Circle Schools, *Shul Almanach* (Yiddish), 1935. Usher Pen, *Yiddishkeit in America* (Yiddish), 1950s.

Labor-Zionist Alliance (575 Sixth Avenue, New York City 10011) should have sources concerning the Shule movement of the Jewish National Labor Alliance (Farband); Itche Goldberg, on the Shules of the Jewish People's Fraternal Order: *Die Ordn Shuln* (Yiddish), *Jewish Secular Education: Its Values and Meaning* (English), and articles in the periodical, *Yiddishe-Kultur.* See also Max Rosenfeld, articles in the periodical *Jewish Currents.*

All these and miscellaneous articles in Yiddish, particularly the early writings of Chaim Zhitlovsky concerning the theoretical base of the *Shule* movement, are on file in the library at YIVO, 1048 Fifth Avenue, New York City.

ONE-ROOM SCHOOLS

Dewey, Evelyn. *New Schools for Old.* New York: Dutton, 1919. See especially the story of Marie Turner Harvey's transformation of a

Bibliography

rural school (Porter School) in Missouri in which the curriculum including the three R's was redesigned out of the life of the community.

Keppel, Ann M. "Country Schools for Country Children: Backgrounds of Reform Movement in Rural Elementary Education, 1890-1914." Doctoral thesis, University of Wisconsin, 1960. Presents the agrarian reform movement in the schools that sounded the common theme that rural education was irrelevant: dealt too much with books, too little with life of the countryside.

Sarton, May. *I Knew a Phoenix*. New York: W. W. Norton, 1959. A description of her early years in the Shady Hill school (then a Cooperative Open Air School), "where children were brought up to be individuals, constantly aware of their relationships to each other and to cherish differences, and experiences were those created out of our several skills and shared together."

Weber, Julia. *The Diary of a Country School Teacher*. 2nd ed., rev. New York: Dell, 1970. An account of her beginning years of teaching in a one-room school in New Jersey.

HIGHLANDER

Adams, Frank. "Highlander Folk School," *Harvard Educational Review*. November 1972.

Adams, Frank and Horton, Myles. *Unearthing Seeds of Fire: The Idea of Highlander*. Winston Salem: John F. Blair, 1975. A history of the development of the Highlander School.

Carawan, Guy and Candie. *Voices from the Mountains: Life and Struggle in the Appalachian South*. New York: Knopf, 1975. A good sociological account of the Appalachian South.

Clark, Septima. *Echo in My Soul*. New York: Dutton, 1962. The autobiography of a black woman who has devoted her life to educational work among the blacks, the NAACP, the Highlander School and the South Christian Leadership Conference. Includes poignant reminiscences of her early life experiences as a young teacher on Johns Island, South Carolina.

Dobbs, Edith. *Face of an Island*. New York: R. L. Bryan, 1970.

Higgs, Robert, and Manning, Ambrose. *Voices from the Hills*. New York: Ungar Publishers, 1975. A book of readings from Southern Appalachia.

Lewis, Claudia. *Children of the Cumberland*. New York: Columbia University Press, 1946. An account that takes in their way of life, with a sensitivity to their differences.

Paulston, Rolland G. *Folk Schools in Social Change*. University

Center for International Studies, 1974. A broad perspective on the folk school movement.

EARLY PROGRESSIVE SCHOOLS

Aiken, Wilfred. *The Story of the Eight Year Study.* New York: McGraw Hill, 1942. A follow-up study of some 1400 students who had attended progressive schools. Redefer, Frederick L. "A Call to the Educators of America," *SR/World,* 7-27-1974. A good article that reexamines this study in the light of current concerns in secondary and higher education.

Alcott, Bronson. *Principles and Methods of Infant Instruction.* Boston: Carter & Hendee, 1830. Describes his school which focused on the child as individual and on a curriculum that supported a child's development.

Clapp, Elsie R. *Schools in Action.* New York: Viking Press, 1939. Description of the life and program in two community-centered schools created by the author in Kentucky and West Virginia— schools where learning and living converged for children, teachers and adults. Additional significant details are found in Clapp, *The Uses of Resources in Education.* New York: Harper, 1952.

Cole, Natalie R. *The Arts in the Classroom.* New York: John Day, 1940. Relates her own personal experiences, supported by many descriptions and illustrations of children's response, and her belief in the child to express in poetry, painting and body his feelings and fantasies.

Dewey, John and Evelyn. *Schools of Tomorrow.* New York: Dutton, 1915. Discusses the challenges facing the schools within the framework of the child's personal development and relation to the community.

Hawkins, Frances P. *The Logic of Action: From a Teacher's Notebook.* New York: Pantheon, 1975. Portrays the sensitive match of deaf children from where they were with the adaptation of the author's role to support their inquiry and action.

Johnson, Marietta. *Thirty Years With an Idea.* University, Alabama: University of Alabama Press, 1974. Recounts the development of the idea that dominated the organization and life of the Organic School at Fairhope, Alabama. The adult's supreme responsibility to supply the right conditions for the growth of the individual child.

Mitchell, Lucy Sprague. *Our Children and Our Schools.* New York: Simon and Schuster, 1951. A good description of what schools are doing to carry out their responsibilities.

Bibliography

Murphy, Lois Barclay. *The Widening World of Childhood.* New York: Basic Books, 1962. A book that sensitively discusses the child's growth and development.

Open Education, the Legacy of the Progressive Movement. Washington, D.C.: 1970 Yearbook of NAEYC. Examines the relationship of open education and progressive education.

Parker, Francis W. *Report of the School Committee of Town of Quincy 1878-1879;* and *Talks on Pedagogics.* New York: E.L. Kellogg, 1894; *Talks on Teaching.* New York: A. S. Barnes, 1883. Sources for Parker's educational philosophy and his work with Chicago Normal (1883-1901), later the Francis W. Parker School, are the *Francis W. Parker Yearbooks, 1912-1920.* See also, Heffron, Ida C. *Francis Wayland Parker.* Los Angeles: I. Deach, 1934. A sensitive appreciation of Parker's philosophy and work written by one of his teachers.

Peabody, Elizabeth. *Record of a School.* University of Chicago, 1835. More about Alcott's school. See also, Cheney, Ednah (ed.) *Louisa May Alcott: Her life, letters & journals.* Boston, 1928. Pages 16-20.

Periodical Sources for the Progressive Education movement (1892-1957): *Yearbooks* of the National Society for the Study of Education: *The Forum; The New Republic; The New Era; The Social Frontier; Frontiers of Democracy.*

"Progressive Education and American Progressivism," *Teachers College Record.* (Vol. LX, 1958-59). Personal experiences by leaders in Progressive Education as well as critiques of the movement.

Snyder, Agnes. *Dauntless Women in Childhood Education 1856-1931.* Washington, D.C.: Association for Childhood Education International, 1972. A valuable compilation of biographies of women who have made valuable contributions to the education of young children.

Study of the 7-Year-Old-Group. New York: Dutton, 1942. An important contribution focusing teachers on close observation of children, on their interactions with each other and adults.

Winsor, Charlotte, ed. *Experimental Schools Revisited.* New York: Agathon Press, 1973. Republication of selected bulletins from the Bureau of Educational Experiments in New York City reflecting approaches to early childhood education, 1917-1924, in some of the best progressive schools.

DAY CARE AND PLAY SCHOOL PROGRAMS

Franklin, Adele. *Play Centers for School Children.* New York: William Morrow, 1943.

Franklin Street Settlement and Day Nursery. Detroit Day Nursery Association, 1932.
Goldsmith, Cornelia. *Better Day Care for the Young Child.* Washington: NAEYC, 1972. A comprehensive history of day care in New York City.
Lies, Eugene T. *The Day Nursery as a Factor in the Problem of Relief and Family Rehabilitation.* Proceedings of National Education Association, 1916.
Miho, Nancy. *9226 Kercheval: the storefront that did not burn.* Ann Arbor, Michigan: University of Michigan Press, 1970. An interesting presentation of a recent storefront program.
Pratt, Caroline. *The Play School, An Experiment in Education.* New York: Bureau of Educational Experiments, Bull. No. 3, Bank Street College of Education, 1917. For her more personal statement of her belief in the child's desire to clarify ideas for himself and her commitment to support for their ways of growing and learning, *I Learn from Children,* New York: Simon and Schuster, 1948.

IMMIGRANT AND ADULT EDUCATION

Black, Algernon D. *The Young Citizens.* New York: Frederick Ungar, 1962. The story and meaning of a unique experiment in preparation for democratic citizenship, as described by its founder.
Borrie. W. D. *The Cultural Integration of Immigrants.* New York: Oxford University Press, 1959. A discussion of the impact of immigration and nationalism on the schools.
Ditzion, Sidney H. *Arsenals of a Democratic Culture: A Social History of the American Public Library Movement in New England and the Middle States, 1850 to 1900.* Chicago: American Library Association, 1947. An interesting history of the cultural forces operating in the growth of the public library, analyzed in terms of the library's function as educator. Alessios, Alison B. *The Greek Immigrant and His Reading.* Chicago: American Library Association, 1926. The response of a particular ethnic group to the public library.
Gordon, Milton. *Assimilation in American Life: The role of race, religion and national origins.* New York: Oxford University Press, 1964. An excellent statement on pluralism in American life.
Hapgood, Hutchins. *The Spirit of the Ghetto.* Reprint. Cambridge: Harvard University Press, 1967. A sympathetic view of life in the Jewish quarter in New York City during the early 1900s. Metzker,

Bibliography

Isaac, ed. *A Bintel Brief: Sixty Years of Letters from the Lower East Side to the Jewish Daily Forward*. New York: Ballantine, 1971. People, who when schools do not meet their needs, ask questions and seek answers—as recorded in the *Jewish Daily Forward*, a daily newspaper in Yiddish.

Riis, Jacob A. *How the Other Half Lives*. Reprint. Cambridge: Harvard University Press, 1970.

Lindeman, Eduard. *The Meaning of Adult Education*. Montreal: Harvest House, 1961. A significant discussion of adult education.

Fisher, Dorothy Canfield. *Why Stop Learning*. New York: Harcourt Brace, 1927. A more personal statement than Lindeman's. Two other strands of informal education for adults are described in: Bode, Carl. *American Lyceum: Town Meeting of the Mind*. Carbondale, Ill.: Southern Illinois University Press, 1968; Case, Robert and Victoria. *We Called It Culture: The Story of Chautauqua*. Plainview, New York: Books for Libraries, 1948; and Morrison, Theodore. *Chautauqua: A Center for Education, Religion, and the Arts in America*. Chicago: University of Chicago Press, 1974.

MISCELLANEOUS ACCOUNTS

Alcott, Louisa May. *Little Men* and *Little Women*.

Flexner, Abraham. *I Remember*. New York: Simon & Schuster, 1946. See particularly the section in which he describes his own teaching as a young man in Louisville, Kentucky, at a school that he organized based on the philosophy of giving children "the knowledge and power to handle themselves in their world."

Franchere, Ruth. *Willa, the Story of Willa Cather Growing Up*. New York: Crowell, 1958. A good portrayal of self-education.

Ritchie, Jean. *Singing Family of the Cumberland*. New York: Oak Publishing, 1963. Self-directed education within a family and the community in the mountains of Appalachia: how family recollections of seven generations were shared, songs and stories remembered.

Tharp, Louise H. *The Peabody Sisters of Salem*. Boston: Little Brown, 1950. The lives of the three Peabody sisters, with emphasis on Elizabeth's constant quest for knowledge, her strong belief in people as individuals, her long life as teacher ending in her establishment of the first kindergarten at Pinckney Street in Boston in 1861, which also served as a training school and discussion center for the ideas of Froebel. See also, Elizabeth Peabody, *Education in the Home, The Kindergarten and the Primary School*. London: Swam, Sonnenschein, Lowry & Co., 1877.

CONTRIBUTORS

MARIAN BROOKS, professor emerita of City University, began her teaching career in a one-room school in northern New Hampshire. She studied at Teachers College with Harold Rugg and George Counts before coming to City College in 1948 where she served as chairman of the Elementary Education department. After her retirement in 1972, she joined the staff of the Workshop Center for Open Education where she serves as consultant.

MARY BURKS was born in Danville, Virginia. Her early education was received in a two-room school in that state. Later she graduated from Virginia State College with a degree in sociology. At present, she is a local advisor for the Follow Through program in Paterson, New Jersey.

H. DANIEL CARPENTER first joined the Hudson Guild Neighborhood House as a staff member in 1931, and became its executive director in 1943, a job he performed for 30 years. He is now executive director emeritus of the Hudson Guild and president of PACT/NADAP, a nonprofit voluntary organization sponsored by business and labor to work on drug abuse problems.

WALTER E. CLARK was born in 1905 on a family farm, grew up in rural western New York, studied at Antioch College in the late 1920s, worked as a camp counselor and teacher throughout the 1930s, and then helped found the North Country (Residential) School at Lake Placid, New York, which he served as co-director until 1970.

LOUIS COHEN was born in 1906, brought up on the Lower East Side of New York, took degrees from City College (B.A.) and Columbia University (M.A.), and taught English in the public schools.

SAKAKOHE COOK was raised on the Mohawk Reserve of Akwesasne. She left to attend high school in Watertown, New York and later, college in Rochester, New York. Since then, she has worked with a number of Native American organizations, including the Rochester Iroquois Youth Council, an organization formed to teach social dances and songs of the Iroquois to the urban Indian youth; the Native American Counseling Center, an alcoholism program in New York City; the Native American Educational Research Program, and the American Indian Community House, Inc.

DOROTHY COTTON graduated from Shaw University in Raleigh, North Carolina. While working as a librarian at Virginia State Col-

Contributors

lege in Petersburg, Virginia and active in the local civil rights movement, she met Martin Luther King, Jr. and became one of the original staff of five when he formed the Southern Christian Leadership Conference. At SCLC, she directed the Citizenship Schools Program. She is now with the Atlanta Department of Community and Human Development.

JOSEPH FEATHERSTONE writes for the *New Republic*, of which he is a contributing editor, and teaches at the Harvard Graduate School of Education. He has written *Schools Where Children Learn* and *What Schools Can Do*, and he is working on a book about John Dewey.

EDWARD GLANNON was born in Pittsburgh in 1911. He became a student at the Art Students League where he studied with Kenneth Hayes Miller and Thomas Benton. His first chance to be a teacher came through the teaching project of the WPA. He taught at Gramercy Boys' Club in the old Gashouse District of New York. Later, he taught at Fieldston, one of the Ethical Culture Society schools, for 26 years. For the last 10 years, he has been associated with the Roslyn, Long Island, public schools, working in the high school and kindergarten.

CORNELIA GOLDSMITH was born in St. Paul, Minnesota, in 1892. A teacher in public and private schools in St. Paul, San Diego and New York City, she was director of the Lower School of the Walden School in New York City from 1931 to 1940. After teaching child development at Vassar, she joined New York City's Health Department to create and direct the city's day care program from 1943 to 1963.

HELEN HALL trained as a social worker, was director of University Settlement in Philadelphia from 1922 to 1933, and then succeeded Lillian Wald as Headworker of the Henry Street Settlement on the Lower East Side of New York.

DAVID HAWKINS was born in El Paso, Texas, in 1913. He took his Ph.D. in philosophy at the University of California, Berkeley, became an instructor of philosophy at Stanford and Berkeley, was project historian for the Los Alamos Laboratory (Manhattan Project) from 1943 to 1946, and in 1947 joined the faculty at the University of Colorado in Boulder, where he is professor of philosophy and director of the Mountain View Center for Environmental Education. From 1962 to 1964, he was also director of the Elementary Science Study in Newton, Massachusetts.

NEITH HEADLEY has taught in both public and private schools and colleges in California, Maine, Massachusetts, Maryland, and

Minnesota. Currently she is the Early Childhood Education Consultant for the Association for Childhood Education International. She is also co-author with Josephine Foster of two volumes dealing with education and observations in the kindergarten, and author of *The Kindergarten: Its Place in the Program of Education.*

MYLES HORTON was born in Savannah, Tennessee, in 1905. After graduate work at the Union Theological Seminary in the late 1920s, where he studied with Reinhold Neibuhr, he founded and was director of the Highlander Folk School in Monteagle, Tennessee, which served the labor union movement in the 1930s and 1940s, and then the civil rights movement in the 1950s and 1960s. Besides being a college lecturer, he has worked as a union organizer and as education director of the United Packinghouse Workers Union.

NEVA LAROCQUE HOWRIGAN received her first schooling in a rural one-room building in Bristol, Vermont, where she was born in 1917. After two years of training at a normal school, she herself became a teacher in a one-room schoolhouse in the neighboring township. At age 24, she married Francis Howrigan and, together, they had 12 children and maintained a farm. She now participates in a special education program in St. Alban's, Vermont.

CLAUDIA LEWIS grew up in Oregon, began her career as a teacher of nursery and primary school children, and from 1938 to 1941 directed and taught a little nursery school for Tennessee mountain children in connection with the Highlander Folk School. Out of this last experience came her book, *Children of the Cumberland,* in 1946.

JULIUS MANSON was a mediator and arbitrator for the New York State Board of Mediation in the 1950s and early 1960s. In 1966-67, he served in Turkey as a labor consultant for A.I.D. He is professor of management at Baruch College of the City University of New York.

PAUL NASH is professor and chairman of the Department of Humanistic and Behavioral Studies at Boston University. English-born, he served as a Royal Air Force pilot in World War II. He is a former school teacher. Trained in economics and history at Queen's University, Belfast, and the London School of Economics, and in teaching at London University Institute of Education, he has held academic posts at numerous universities here and abroad, and is the author of several works, including *Authority and Education* (1966).

Contributors

VITO PERRONE has been Dean of the Center for Teaching and Learning at the University of North Dakota since 1968.

OSBORNE E. SCOTT is professor of Black Studies at the City College of New York and acting director of Africa House, the college's center for both African students and scholars and the study of African culture.

MARK STARR worked in the mines of South Wales and wrote three widely-used labor textbooks before coming to the United States in 1928. He taught British Labor History at Brookwood Labor College and later became its extension director. He was director of the Educational Department of the International Ladies Garment Workers Union from 1935 to 1960.

LILLIAN WEBER is professor of Elementary Education at the School of Education, City College of New York. She is the founder and director of the Workshop for Open Education (since 1972) and of the City College Advisory Service to Open Corridors (since 1970). She is the author of the basic book on the practice and theory of open education, *The English Infant School And Informal Education* (Prentice-Hall, 1971).

CHARLOTTE WINSOR'S professional experience in education began with a student year at the City and Country School in the years when it was closely affiliated with the Bureau of Educational Experiments, the organization which later became Bank Street College. At Bank Street College, she was chairman of the Graduate Programs Division and for some years, director of the Bank Street Workshops in the New York City public schools. Still active at Bank Street, she is the College's Distinguished Teacher and Education Specialist Emerita.

VINCENT WRIGHT taught in the New York City public schools from 1961 to 1966. Since then he has been an assistant professor and assistant dean of students at Virginia Commonwealth University, director of the Second Chance Program at Virginia Union University, and assistant director of education at Lincoln Center. He is currently associate director of the Panel of Americans of the National Conference of Christians and Jews where he directs the Encampment for Citizenship program.